STEALTH WAR

STEALTH WAR

HOW CHINA TOOK OVER WHILE AMERICA'S ELITE SLEPT

BRIGADIER GENERAL **Robert Spalding**
(US AIR FORCE, RETIRED)
WITH **Seth Kaufman**

PORTFOLIO / PENGUIN

Portfolio / Penguin
An imprint of Penguin Random House LLC
penguinrandomhouse.com

Most Portfolio books are available at a discount when purchased in quantity for sales promotions or corporate use. Special editions, which include personalized covers, excerpts, and corporate imprints, can be created when purchased in large quantities. For more information, please call (212) 572-2232 or email specialmarkets@penguinrandomhouse.com. Your local bookstore can also assist with discounted bulk purchases using the Penguin Random House corporate Business-to-Business program. For assistance in locating a participating retailer, email B2B@penguinrandomhouse.com.

ISBN 9780593084342 (hardcover)
ISBN 9780593084359 (ebook)

Printed in the United States of America
5 7 9 10 8 6 4

BOOK DESIGN BY TANYA MAIBORODA

To all who have pledged their life, liberty, and sacred honor to preserve our Republic

CONTENTS

PREFACE

KNOWLEDGE IN THE WEST IS BUILT ON A FOUNDATION of documented facts. The historical record has been filled with the accounts and chronicles of nations built on a foundation of law. In the United States, the Freedom of Information Act ensures the disclosure, at some point, of information controlled by the US government.

But how do you document the history and governance of a nation that does not subscribe to the conventions of the West? What if such a nation is not eager to see their secrets revealed? What if they are not subject to government-disclosure rules? For too long, I've borne the burden of stories about the Chinese Communist Party (CCP) and the awareness that their system ensures that secrets stay buried.

This book is my attempt to enter those stories into the record. My hope is that, by doing so, others will be willing to come forward on the record also, as the risks to their lives and fortunes will be mitigated by our slow disengagement from the CCP.

Of course, there is another possibility. If we do not

disengage, then we will become ever more constrained in our speech and freedoms as the CCP seeks to suppress the knowledge of our own history. If this comes to pass, this book and indeed the Constitution will have little relevance.

Because I wanted to make this book as user-friendly as possible, and because I conducted hundreds of interviews, many of which required confidentiality, I have opted to dispense with endnotes. This book represents only a fraction of what I've learned, but it was written to address an urgent need: to bring the stealth war into public view. It was never intended to be an encyclopedia.

I leave it to future patriots to delve deeper and document the mysteries of the CCP, to provide a basis of knowledge, and to aid the continuation of our Republic and the freedom it guarantees.

INTRODUCTION

I KNOW SOMETHING ABOUT STEALTH. IN 1998, I BEgan training to pilot B-2 Spirits, known far and wide as Stealth Bombers. The B-2 was at that time the high-profile new weapon in the US Air Force arsenal, a dazzling, billion-dollar, high-tech machine that looked like it had flown in from a future century. Its "continuous curvature" allowed it to avoid detection by the electromagnetic waves used by radar systems to track objects. In other words, I learned to fly a plane that achieved something every military strategist has dreamed of: being invisible.

Twenty years later—having served as chief China strategist for the chairman of the Joint Chiefs of Staff and as senior US Defense official and Defense attaché to the People's Republic of China—I left my position as senior director for strategic planning at the White House, deeply concerned about a different stealth weapon being turned against my country. For the past forty years, the Chinese Communist Party (CCP) has been playing a beautiful game. It is sophisticated yet simple. It is a competition to gain control and influence across the planet—and to achieve that outcome without resorting to military engagement.

Flying quietly below the radar, the CCP has been acquiring technology without paying a cent toward developing it, carefully taking control of the world's shipping businesses, infiltrating our corporations and science laboratories, and using American investor dollars to float the cost of its own factories and companies—and then, adding insult to injury, insisting that that money stay in China.

War between nation-states in the twenty-first century looks much different than war in the nineteenth and twentieth centuries. Instead of bombs and bullets, it's about ones and zeros and dollars and cents: economics, finance, data information, manufacturing, infrastructure, and communications. Control those fronts today, and you can win a war without firing a shot. It's a simple, logical strategy. And it is one leaders in the West have been very slow to grasp.

Our political, military, corporate, and fiscal leaders have failed to recognize the subtle game the CCP has been playing. They have been operating, understandably, under the now outdated idea that war is fought only with bombs and bullets. The CCP strategy, however, is to fight in other ways, utilizing a variety of tactics. It advocates and sponsors a constant focus on theft, coercion, economic sabotage, and monopolization of infrastructure on a global level—all to increase China's sphere of influence. Everywhere.

Like the B-2 bombers I flew, the CCP's stealth war isn't

truly covert. It has been hiding in plain sight. How did we miss it? I'm not interested in pointing fingers at one particular party. Both Republican and Democratic elites have missed the signs—or are complicit—and as a patriot who cares about my fellow citizens, my main interest is to defend the people of this country and the ideas that have driven it since it was founded.

Perhaps nothing threatens the CCP more than the Constitution of the United States. China's president, Xi Jinping, has stated as much, and CCP documents that I will share make clear that fundamental American concepts—the rights of free speech and freedom of religion—are threats to the authoritarian power of the CCP, which believes that these liberties must *never* be allowed to take root in China and must never be the rights of Chinese citizens.

The CCP's fundamental loathing of our Bill of Rights and other legal protections should be chilling to anyone who values freedom. It is the primary reason I am writing this book. I want to alert the world to China's stealth war and its strategy to dominate the planet by focusing on six spheres of influence: the economy, the military, global diplomacy, technology, education, and infrastructure.

China is closing in on achieving its goal of influencing the politicians and corporations of the United States. If this happens, fundamental freedoms we take for granted—the ability to criticize a politician or a policy, to publish political statements, to report on governmental abuse or inefficiency, to sing the lyrics you want, to study literally any subject under the sun, to visit any website, no matter what ideology is espoused—will come under assault.

As for our economy, it will continue to erode, as the CCP arranges to use our own capital against our own best interests. Trade terms will be less favorable. Chinese-owned and -manufactured products will flood our markets, creating a further trade imbalance that will favor the CCP's interests. The job market and average wages will continue to stagnate. Our best and brightest will be recruited by Chinese-owned companies—which are, as we'll see, ultimately property of the CCP.

American politicians who attempt to counter pro-CCP rivals will find themselves fighting against operatives who are bought and paid for, as the CCP uses its limitless cash to influence policies in Washington, DC.

Equally frightening, if not more so, the CCP is also using its authoritarian power to reshape, rewrite, and airbrush historical truths—earning the nation a joke moniker among academics who study the disturbing manipulation of historical fact: The People's Republic of Amnesia. The era of digitization makes editing history and creating national amnesia a matter of just cutting, pasting, and deleting. A fascinating study by Glenn Tiffert, "Peering Down the Memory Hole," documents how past issues of China's leading law journals were published on Chinese digital platforms for academic research, but without specific articles within them that revealed attacks on the concept of rule of law. Those attacks presented an inconvenient truth now that China seeks to portray itself as law-abiding and just. So they were banished. "Simply put," writes Tiffert, "the Chinese government is leveraging technology to quietly export its domestic censorship regime abroad and, by manipulating how observers everywhere comprehend its past, present, and future, it is enlisting them without their consent in an alarming project to sanitize the historical record and globalize its own competing narratives."

The end result, if China succeeds in all its goals, will be a United States of America that is devoid of the principles that shaped our nation.

These are the dystopian outcomes that loom before us. It is not a question of *if.* It is a question of *when*, unless we take preventative measures. The strategies the CCP deploys across the globe have been in effect for decades. And under its current power-hungry leader Xi Jinping, it is trying to accelerate influencing operations by attempting to become the world's technology leader, corner the telecommunications market, and export totalitarian social controls to the leaders in developing nations.

This book does not aim to just sound an alarm. It is meant as a call to arms, one that details how the United States and the rest of the free world can combat—and break up—China's stealth war. In doing so, I hope we can save the very thing that has driven our nation—and the world—forward for nearly 250 years, a shared value of what Franklin Delano Roosevelt and Winston Churchill termed the four essential liberties in the Atlantic Charter: freedom of speech, freedom of religion, freedom from want, and freedom from fear.

So consider this book a primer on how the CCP has conducted its war, a point-by-point how-to manual for stopping its march toward control of the West, and, yes, a terrifying warning. If we fail to respond immediately and decisively to protect our economy, our security, our institutions, and our free society, we will descend, as much of China already has, into a nightmarish dystopian society. A foreign totalitarian state will monitor our lives, our thoughts, who we see, and what we say. And if it doesn't like what we do or think or say, it will take action against us.

Some cynics will accuse me of being alarmist or sensationalist. These people are afflicted with the same blind spot I once had. I have examined why I was so oblivious to CCP aggression and why the rest of the world still has a similar blind spot. I now attribute it in part to hubris—our cocksure confidence in ourselves and our system. Our belief that America's socioeconomic model, its war machine, and its political model are the best in the world has helped fuel a profound confidence that we can overcome any challenge. That confidence has proven shortsighted. The blind spot remains in place—and has increased in size—because the CCP are professional liars who have had exquisite training.

Blinded by our own greed and the dream of globalization, we've been convinced that free trade automatically unlocks the shackles of authoritarianism and paves the way to democracy. The promise of cheap labor, inexpensive goods, and soaring stock prices has been spellbinding, but by giving up our manufacturing expertise and dominance, we have given up our independence and sold out our own citizens by stripping them of work. And we've been duped: investing in an authoritarian nation that insists the money never leave the country is basically allowing our pockets to be picked—or, rather, allowing our treasury to be raided.

America, other Western nations, and all democratic countries now face our biggest challenge since World War II—one with dire implications for the United States and the world at large. I hope this book—and the much-needed response I pray it spurs—is not too late to stop the authoritarian juggernaut, the stealth war, that is being waged against us.

STEALTH WAR

CHAPTER ONE

UNRESTRICTED WARFARE

OVER THE COURSE OF ABOUT TWELVE MONTHS BE-tween 2016 and 2017, I wooed a major Washington, DC, think tank. My goal was to get the organization to conduct a study on the Chinese Communist Party's influence in the corporate sector of the United States. I wanted a respected, nonpartisan institution to shine a light on the CCP's operations. How did Chinese diplomats, investors, and businessmen seek to manipulate our captains of industry? Were they building alliances with board members? What business segments did they value the most? Just how inextricably entrenched had they become in American business? And most important, had they succeeded in making US companies act in ways that ultimately served China's interests, not ours?

My courtship was calculated. The think tank had been

rated among the top five in the United States. It was respected and revered for strategic policy work in politics, international trade, and national security. I had several meetings to discuss the project and was convinced everything was on track. We discussed how important this study would be. How it would turn the corporate and investment world on its head. How it might possibly lead to much-needed policy and national security reforms. In the ultimate declaration of intent when it comes to cash-conscious think tanks, I even arranged for donors to pay for the study. Conducting the study wouldn't cost the organization a dime.

My campaign gained traction. I had a compelling idea for a study of national importance. I had found the money to pay for it. And so, one Friday, I received word that the head of the institute agreed to green-light the study. I was elated.

Three days later, on Sunday evening, the think tank president, a quintessential Beltway insider who had vaulted from governmental appointments to his current position of power and influence, called the donors for the project.

"I'm not sure the study is the right fit for us," he told them. He was pulling the plug.

He didn't give any other explanation. But once I looked at the board of trustees for his organization, I knew the reason behind the decision. His benefactors were a who's who of China-loving Washington and Wall Street elites, including at least one world-famous figure, and a slew of investment house billionaires. The study wasn't the right fit because the people who raised money for the think tank were profiting off of China. They are the same people who refuse to confront China despite the onslaught of horror stories coming from within its borders and hard-to-miss headlines about organ harvesting from prisoners, herding two million members of the Muslim Uighur population into concentration camps, and unilaterally pushing to deprive millions of citizens of Hong Kong of their civil rights.

This think tank incident was not an isolated case.

When I got to the White House in 2017 as a member of the National Security Council (NSC), I made it a personal mission to meet with many leading think tanks, nongovernmental organizations, and law, auditing, and public relations firms that dealt with China. I was eager to seek their help in exposing the Beijing government's influencing operations and sanctioning of illegal behavior. Additionally, I hoped they would help me explore policy options to counter China's economic malfeasance.

Time after time, I was rebuffed.

People at these organizations would talk with me, and many of them even said they agreed with my concerns, but they claimed they couldn't help. Doing so, some of the more forthright people said, might anger their Chinese funders or business accounts. The list of organizations that refused to engage with me publicly in my official capacity was stunning. Top white-shoe New York law firms. Organizations with mandates to promote democracy, freedom, and human rights would refuse to support my mission.

The irony of this wasn't lost on me. I was determined to

educate America about how China uses money to influence governments and institutions around the world to shape political and economic outcomes to their advantage. But because those same institutions were already under the influence of that money, they were terrified of losing donations or business income if they helped me expose the CCP's strategy.

They were, in essence, being manipulated by a foreign power that is America's greatest enemy.

I originally suspected that the CCP's conspiracy to infiltrate the United States was actually an *alliance* between American elites and the CCP. Many of our political leaders regard China as a partner, despite the fact that the CCP has declared itself at war with the West. American power brokers just don't realize what getting rich off Chinese investments in the short term means for us in the long term. Our intricate relations with China should alarm and frighten patriots of all political persuasions.

This alliance is nonpartisan: major figures on the right and on the left have fallen for the short-term gains of involvement with China. One surprising player is Senate Majority Leader Mitch McConnell, a known opponent of Trump's protectionist instincts, whose family has strong ties to the most powerful people in China. In 1993, McConnell married Elaine Chao, George W. Bush's Labor secretary and current secretary of Transportation. Her father, James Chao, a scion of a powerful shipping family, attended Shanghai Jiao Tong University with Jiang Zemin, the general secretary of the Chinese Communist Party from 1989 to 2002. James Chao moved his family to Taiwan and then to the United States, where in 1964 he founded the Foremost Group, a shipping, trading, and finance firm. He and his old schoolmate Jiang stayed in contact. When Jiang became mayor of Shanghai, Chao reportedly placed an order for two ships to be built at the state-owned shipyard there. According to the May 16, 2001, issue of the *South China Morning Post*, the two men would meet regularly, and "Mr. Chao's business ties to Beijing would deepen as he started chartering his ships to mainland giants, such as Cosco and Sinotrans."

This connection is highly disturbing. Elaine Chao's family members—including her father, James, and her sister, Angela, now the CEO of Foremost—have donated at least $1 million to McConnell's campaigns over the years, the *New York Times* reported in a June 2, 2019, article that explored how the Chao family has benefited from business with China. And according to McConnell's 2008 Senate Financial Disclosure Report, he and his wife received a gift of between $5 million and $25 million. A McConnell spokesman told the press the windfall was an inheritance from Chao's late mother. As Kathleen Clark, a law professor and anticorruption expert at Washington University in St. Louis, told *The New York Times*, "This is a family with financial ties to a government that is a strategic rival. It raises a question about whether those familial and financial ties affect Chao when she exercises judgment or gives advice on foreign and national security policy matters that involve China."

Meanwhile, McConnell has evidently developed close personal ties, as well. The 2001 *South China Morning Post* report reads, "Ms. Chao and Mr. McConnell married in February 1993, and in December the pair met Mr. Jiang in Beijing, joined by Ms. Chao's father."

Mitch McConnell's father-in-law is a man who has made untold millions. It seems likely he made those millions in part through his relationship with the general secretary of China. Meanwhile, in 2016, just days after Trump was elected president, the board of directors at the Bank of China announced that McConnell's sister-in-law, Angela Chao, had been appointed a "non-executive director of the bank." This marked her second major appointment in China, having previously served—along with her dad—on the board of CSSC Holdings, according to author Peter Schweizer's book *Secret Empires.* CSSC, by the way, stands for China State Shipbuilding Corporation, the largest defense contractor in China. It's alarming to think that our Senate leader's sister-in-law meets with the corporate leaders of America's number-one business adversary—and sits on the board of its national bank.

This should be a major concern to anyone who believes in good governance, but it's precisely the kind of access the CCP dreams of for its influencing operations. Did anyone in G. W. Bush's administration wonder about the fact that its secretary of Labor, Elaine Chao—who served in a time when millions of jobs began vanishing from US soil—just happened to be a family friend of the president of China?

What's worse, the daughter of a man who made millions shipping goods from China while befriending the president of China is now overseeing US transportation. This is distressing, considering that China now seeks to control the world's shipping and aviation industries. Her own family's ties to China—financial, historical, and emotional—leave her and her husband open to possible manipulation.

Democrats are just as tainted. According to *Secret Empires*, Hunter Biden, the son of former vice president Joe Biden, teamed up with the Bank of China to create a $1 billion investment fund called Bohai Harvest RST. Schweizer reveals that in early December 2013, Hunter Biden flew with his father on *Air Force Two* to China. While the vice president was meeting with CCP leaders, Hunter may have had some meetings of his own; approximately ten days after the trip to Beijing, the deal for a billion in funds "backed by the Chinese government" was finalized. A July 7, 2019, *New Yorker* article reported that "the deal had been signed before the trip" and a business license "came through shortly afterward." Everything about the deal—the players involved, the timing, the amount of cash—reeks of undue influence on the part of both China and the profiteering son of a premier power broker.

As Schweizer wrote in a May 11, 2019, op-ed piece for the *New York Post*, "It was an unprecedented arrangement: the government of one of America's fiercest competitors going into business with the son of one of America's most powerful decision makers."

Amazingly, Joe Biden doesn't seem to have any issues with his son's choice of business partners or the inescapable negative optics—of potential bribery, of purchasing access, of elite privilege, not to mention the misuse of *Air Force Two*—created by such deals. But then Biden has been a China cheerleader for decades, actively pushing to pass permanent national trade relations with China in 2001. Recent comments Biden has made on the campaign trail reveal that he remains utterly clueless about China's strategic long game against the West. "China is going to eat our lunch? Come on, man," he said. "They can't even figure out how to deal with the fact that they have this great division between the China Sea and the mountains in the . . . west. They can't figure out how they're going to deal with the corruption that exists within the system. . . . They're not bad folks, folks, but guess what? They're not competition for us."

When a nation gives your son and his partners a billion dollars to invest, I guess it's hard to think of them as competition. But tricking America into this kind of short-term thinking is all a part of China's ultimate strategy.

This is how dangerously entrenched and intertwined China has become with America's political elite. But China has equally hypnotized the so-called wizards of Wall Street. The heads of major investment houses have become some of China's most vocal cheerleaders. Blackstone Group CEO Stephen Schwarzman and Ray Dalio, cochairman of the massive Bridgewater hedge fund, have consistently portrayed China as an unquestionably positive economic force. Their bullish attitude is understandable as far as their own profit motives are concerned. The fees generated on trillions of dollars of trades and bonds are astounding: the research division of the Federal Bank of St. Louis put the total 2017 revenue of all securities brokerages at $147,917,000,000. So promoting the trade of Chinese stocks and bonds adds to brokerage earnings. China also often serves as both a Wall Street backer and a client. Dow Jones reports that Chinese firms—including the China Investment Corporation and the State Administration of Foreign Exchange, both government agencies—have invested billions in Bridgewater's existing hedge funds.

The tech world has also been targeted by CCP tactics. Ray Bingham—formerly a board member of tech giant Oracle and executive chairman of US chip maker Cypress Semiconductor Corporation—was hired in 2016 by Canyon Bridge, a private equity company funded by China Reform Fund Management, a Chinese state-owned investment firm. According to a letter to Cypress stockholders, Bingham received a $1.2 million signing bonus from Canyon Bridge, $2 million in salary, "plus his 'carried interest' of 20% of Canyon Bridge's profits." ("Carried interest" is a term specifying that a partner will get a commission regardless of whether he contributed to a deal in any way.) By hiring someone with Bingham's savvy and understanding of technology, China found yet another point man to guide strategic acquisitions and funnel key technology to China. And, as expected, Bingham's first move was to try to purchase his former company—a deal that was stopped because of national security concerns.

These are just a few high-profile examples of how China connects with America's elite, the people who make policy and monetary decisions for our nation and around the globe. They have fostered engagement with China. And those decisions have had a direct, brutal impact on American citizens.

Simply put, 3.4 million US jobs vanished between 2001 and 2017 due to our trade relationship with China, according to "The China Toll Deepens," a 2018 study by the Economic Policy Institute (EPI). China joined the World Trade Organization (WTO) in 2001. Since that time, according to the EPI, America's growing trade deficit has swelled, and the impact of that imbalance has been cataclysmic. The study found that nearly 75 percent of the jobs lost between 2001 and 2017—2.5 million (calculated by subtracting the number of job opportunities lost to imports from the number of jobs created by exports)—were in manufacturing. That's a staggering number of Americans—roughly the equivalent of the population of Houston—who have been put out of work. When Americans think of bad times, they think of the Great Depression, but according to the Information Technology & Innovation Foundation, in the 2000s, "the decline [in manufacturing jobs (5.7 million)] as a share of total manufacturing jobs (33 percent) exceeded the rate of loss in the Great Depression [30.9 percent]."

The EPI study is filled with other disturbing numbers, including a finding that trade deficits with China between 2001 and 2011 reduced the incomes of directly impacted US workers by $37 billion per year. The report also contains many concise insights about China's "trade-distorting practices"—such as "extending large subsidies to industries such as steel, glass, paper, concrete, and renewable energy industries and rapidly growing its state-owned enterprises, both of which generated a massive buildup of excess capacity in a range of these sectors. This excess capacity created a supply of goods far exceeding Chinese consumer demand, and China dealt with the oversupply by dumping the exports elsewhere, primarily in the United States."

The political leaders and financial elite I've mentioned here all share one thing in common: they have been operating under a false assumption that our interactions with China are just part of a normal free-market competition. They have failed to realize that the Chinese Communist Party has not played by the rules of international law; instead, it has been conducting a war—one that we have been losing steadily for decades. As a result, our citizens, our cities, and our nation have been gravely wounded. The risks to our nation are increasing, rather than decreasing, every minute we turn a blind eye to China's theft of billions of dollars' worth of intellectual property and technology; to years of piracy and copyright law violations; to the CCP's closed economy, the artificial valuation of its own currency, its relentless political influencing operations; and so much more. As we continue to turn a blind eye, our nation moves closer to losing its independence and its freedom.

They fail, in other words, to realize that we are losing the stealth war.

Unrestricted Warfare

The Chinese Communist Party's ultimate goal—which even the most powerful and well-connected are clueless of or complicit in—is to strengthen itself at every turn. The CCP believes that its biggest obstacle, and indeed, its greatest threat, is the United States of America inasmuch as it remains the global economic and military leader. The party's goal and biggest challenge is to displace America's position on the world stage; the CCP's own documents state as much.

Perhaps the most important and revealing of these documents is a 1999 work called *Unrestricted Warfare.* Written by two senior colonels in China's People's Liberation Army (PLA), Qiao Liang and Wang Xiangsui, it outlined a number of strategies to tilt the balance of power throughout the globe in China's favor. It should be required reading for all branches of the US government and for business leaders, because it outlines, in no uncertain terms, the strategy behind China's policies in the world. Here is a short, chilling passage:

> The new principles of war are no longer "using armed force to compel the enemy to submit to one's will," but rather are "using all means, including armed force or non-armed force, military and non-military, and lethal and non-lethal means to compel the enemy to accept one's interests."

Unrestricted Warfare is not fun, light reading. It is dense, complex reading material that combines strategy and economics, social theory and trenchant observations on technology. It is, however, brilliant, and arguably the most important philosophical and strategic book about warfare of our generation. It was first published in China and widely read within the CCP. Among modern-day China scholars, it is well-known. But perhaps because of its strange complexity, the West has failed to connect its strategic musings with China's often misleadingly benign and smiling diplomacy.

What the CCP realizes, and what *Unrestricted Warfare* lays out, is that a nation no longer needs a vast army in order to conquer—to control another country's population, its resources, or its government. Military might is only one way to express aggression, only one of many ways to attain power. In China's view, economic power strengthens all the fields of potential engagement. In other words, money bolsters the military, but it also bolsters every other sphere of engagement imaginable. It can be used to influence and sway political leaders in foreign countries, silence ideas, and purchase or steal technology. It can be used to manufacture goods at dirt-cheap prices and drive competitors out of business or weaken rival economies. It can be used to create an army of academics, who fan out to gather scientific, technological, and engineering intelligence that can be used to further other goals.

It becomes clear, viewed from the calculating perspective of *Unrestricted Warfare*, that our leaders failed to understand that CCP leaders are merely paying lip service to free trade and globalization while blatantly ignoring the laws governing free trade. China welcomes investment, but it won't let investors take their profits out of the country. Chinese companies set up shop all around the world, but the totalitarian CCP puts all kinds of limits on foreign companies growing in China.

Since the end of the Cold War, leaders in the West have operated under an economic theory that free markets lead to greater wealth. This concept has merged with something called the theory of modernization, a sociological idea asserting that democracy is the direct result of economic growth. As Seymour Lipset, one of the proponents of this theory, put it, "The more well-to-do a nation, the greater the chances that it will sustain democracy."

In other words, free trade leads to wealth, and wealth leads to democracy. This is the idea behind Thomas Friedman's book *The World Is Flat.* And it was the theory that led America's elites to partner with the Chinese Communist Party.

See, America's elites understood the power of the world order created by Winston Churchill and Franklin Delano Roosevelt in a document that still serves as the template for that order as we know it. The Atlantic Charter—all of one page—lays out the principles that would govern international behavior for the next seventy-plus years and underpin other well-known institutions like the United Nations and the WTO.

While the charter has eight paragraphs, there are essentially four principles that govern the international system: 1) free markets, 2) democratic principles, 3) rule of law, and 4) self-determination. It was these four principles that America's elites believed would lead to China's eventual democratization.

Unfortunately, Lipset and so many others in the West failed to understand the intractable nature of the totalitarian Chinese Communist Party, which regards democracy as a fundamental threat to its existence and figured out a way to game the free-market system. The CCP believed that it could turn the tables on the West by convincing Western leaders that it agreed with the principles of the world order while systematically working to undermine them all.

In 2017, when Chinese president Xi Jinping went to the annual World Economic Forum—the epicenter of globalization—in Davos, Switzerland, he said, "We must remain committed to developing global free trade and investment, promote trade and investment liberalization and facilitation through opening-up, and say no to protectionism."

It sounds like he is adopting the West's point of view, but here is where the CCP turns the tables, and why its influence is so subtle, cunning, and effective.

Let me explain. In aerial combat, pilots talk about creating a shared mental model with the other aircraft crew members. This allows for perfect choreography when communication is not possible in a combat environment. In order to achieve a shared mental model, it is not sufficient to just understand the words. Our intent—what we want to achieve and how we are going to react to make our plans a reality—must be crystal clear.

In Davos, the audience heard the words coming out of Xi's mouth, but they did not hear or understand Xi's ultimate intent. They believed that Xi's words meant that he agreed to the underlying principles of globalization—and that is what he wanted them to hear. But when one parses what he actually said and what was left unsaid, it becomes clear Xi offered no firm commitment to anything. There is no mention of adhering to international law, no mention of changing monetary policy to allow for the free flow of earnings out of China. To whom is Xi saying "no to protectionism"? Not China—*everything* about economic policy in China is protectionist. He's saying the West should not be protectionist, because that serves CCP goals. So, in fact, the leader of China was subtly undermining the laws of free trade and globalization while appearing to agree with them.

Xi and the CCP have crafted a shrewd strategy, and they have had the perfect unwitting allies in this scheme: America's elites. By now you've probably guessed what happens in aerial combat when the team doesn't share the correct mental model: chaos. The same can be said for the world order that exists today, and that's the reason for this book.

What Xi was actually saying at Davos was that he needed the West to stay open for business. While he was professing agreement with prevailing Western economic and social theory, he was actually operating on CCP theory. Instead of free trade leading to wealth and wealth leading to democracy, his mental model said globalization and the internet enable the CCP to gain power at the West's expense, by accessing Western money to fund China's economic, military, and technological growth and thereby increasing his nation's power and influence across the globe.

By hijacking the mental model of America's elites, by selling them a fraudulent dream of free trade on a level playing field, Xi could essentially co-opt them, luring them into a game of subterfuge. More important, since the CCP controls China's purse strings, he could set the incentives so that his allies got rich supporting China's power grab.

It is in essence the perfect strategy: promise your enemy short-term profits, and enlist them to help make your country the most powerful in the world. America's elites have been jumping at the chance to join the bandwagon for over forty years, as if it were a dream come true: get rich while making the world safe for democracy.

Fortunately, one thing was standing in the way: the US Constitution, which guarantees our citizens freedoms, including the right to vote—a concept the totalitarian CCP can never imagine. The 3.4 million Americans unemployed by China's great game, along with many of their families and friends, decided they had had enough. Economic and social theory be damned; they were going to make their voices heard. And some of our leaders heard them. We saw this begin to play out in the 2016 national election, as candidates from both sides of the political spectrum, Democrat Bernie Sanders and Republican Donald Trump, began speaking to those who have been abandoned and victimized by unfair free trade—the "China Shock" to our economy. We also saw this in the 2018 midterm elections, as politicians adopted platforms that called for providing more support—higher minimum wages, improved health care—for those abandoned as their jobs were taken overseas.

This book is for and about the men and women of America who yearn for the better life they had before their elites welcomed their enemy into the WTO and into their lives. The following chapters tell the story about where their country has gone wrong and how to get it back on track. And yes, that story is about China's stealth war—the manipulation and duping of America's elites, while hugely important, is only one aspect of a multipronged, relentless offensive—but it is also about America winning that war. About forming a more perfect union, establishing justice, and ensuring domestic tranquility. About providing for the common defense and promoting the general welfare.

Mostly, though, it's about preventing a dystopian future and securing the blessings of liberty for ourselves and for generations to come. The fact is, we have about three years to stop the CCP's unrestricted war. If we don't, the ideals of liberty that have shaped America—our defining concepts of freedom and independence—will face almost certain destruction at the hands of a totalitarian government that values nothing more than its own power.

That power is targeting our country in ways that affect everyone at every level. When China succeeds in luring US investment dollars, those are dollars that are not being invested domestically. That is capital that is leaving America that could have been invested in America, that could have been used to generate jobs here. When a Chinese company pirates an electronic device developed in the United States by an American company and then sells that knockoff device, it is stealing income from the company that invested in creating the device. That loss of income has further repercussions, which can translate into loss of jobs, loss of tax revenue, and loss of future earnings. The CCP's actions and inactions don't just hurt a corporation or a manufacturer. They are attacks on our society as a whole.

The average American citizen needs to understand this.

CHAPTER TWO

HOW WE GOT HERE

THE MAGNITUDE AND COMPLEXITY OF THE STEALTH war that the Chinese Communist Party initiated against the United States and the rest of the Western world is so great that even a close observer of today's headlines will have difficulty grasping it. China's stealth war reaches back not months or years into the past, but centuries. They've been refining their view of history, strategic culture, and political philosophy for much longer than the United States or even the West as we know it today have been around. If we continue to ignore our differences with China that are at the root of the stealth war, we'll continue to lose.

In Western democracies, we have rule of law. Leaders are elected by the people to make laws. Government institutions codify, implement, and enforce the laws. The law is the highest power in the land. There are, ideally, checks and balances and oversight to ensure that the laws are followed.

In China, there is rule by law. Unlike the United States, where all citizens have due process, which guarantees they have legal rights that must be honored by the state, and where we have carefully defined laws to establish, administer, and change legislation, the CCP makes the laws, and the people of China have no say in the matter. The law rules them. There is no recourse. The CCP defines the law and citizens have no way to challenge the law. Nothing, therefore, is more powerful than the Chinese Communist Party.

What drives the CCP? What is the model it relies on to sustain this authoritarian party? And how can a nation even conceive of such a long-term plan and then steer that course? The answer lies in China's history, its strategic culture, and its view of power and competition.

China's strategic culture is intertwined with Confucian ideas of hierarchy, harmony, and responsibility, and mixed with pragmatic views on how power, wealth, and influence can be attained. Time is a living element with ebbs and flows. Outcomes that maximize the benefit for the majority and ignore the wishes of the minority are pursued. Use of military force is viewed not as a means to an end but as a necessity. Economic relationships, financial competition, and the use of information help create influence. And influence is the next best thing to actual power.

China has a 5,000 year history of empire building. Dynasties rose; dynasties fell. Many were complex, far-reaching, all-powerful societies that are among the biggest empires the world has ever seen. In roughly 770 BC, the golden era of China ended, giving way to the years known as the Spring and Autumn Period, followed by the Warring States Period. Various leaders and armies engaged in complex subterfuge, tenuous alliances, secret missions, and cold-blooded betrayals, all in the name of consolidating power and control. Like *Game of Thrones*, but real.

During the Spring and Autumn Period, philosopher Confucius had a huge impact on Chinese culture. A teacher, judge, and minister of justice, he believed in the transformative power of education and the obligation of teachers and students to improve society.

The political events of the Warring States Period helped shape what has become China's best-known book in the West: *The Art of War*, by a military strategist named Sun Tzu. Countless generations of military officers all over the world have studied this book. But so have diplomats, philosophers, and businessmen. This wide appeal is a testament to the genius of Sun Tzu's work; for a book on warfare, it spends a lot of time discussing how to advance national interests—or any interest, really—without actually going to war. Sun Tzu implies that the Chinese society values rigorous, cutthroat competition as a means of advancing goals without creating the risk of actual combat.

Given these foundational texts, is it any surprise that more than two thousand years after Sun Tzu put his ideas to paper, this strategy of war without actual combat to further national goals is in full effect?

The Battle Begins

After Mao Zedong rose to power in 1949, ending a grueling civil war and launching the People's Republic of China and the CCP, a plan began to take root for the nation to embark on a "hundred-year marathon." As amorphous as it was ambitious, the undetailed plan was to return China to its "proper" place in the world as a great empire. Providing added motivation to Mao and his impoverished nation was a desire for vengeance against the current world order. Mao viewed the lowlights inflicted upon China over the previous one hundred years—the British Navy destroying its ports to win the Opium Wars, the collapse of the Qing Dynasty in 1912, and Japan's seizures of Korea and Manchuria—as a "century of humiliation." The CCP continues to foster resentment over these national humiliations by treating them as unhealed wounds and indoctrinating students about them in all grade levels, from kindergarten through university.

The start of the marathon was not easy. There was painfully slow growth. China aligned itself with its totalitarian cousin, the Soviet Union, which itself had limited resources and productivity. In 1958, Mao initiated the Great Leap Forward, a plan to industrialize China and reshape agrarian practices. The program backfired when drought, lack of productivity, and faulty planning led to the four-year-long Great Famine, which left tens of millions dead.

In 1966, Mao used the CCP to launch the so-called Cultural Revolution—a brutal purge designed to rid the population of traditional Chinese and capitalist ways. Teachers, businessmen, intelligentsia, religious leaders, and civil servants were jailed and sent to reeducation camps. Citizens were denounced and publicly humiliated. Property was seized. Populations were forcibly relocated. Torture, executions, and even mass murder were common—millions perished.

The terror of the Cultural Revolution—communist totalitarian government run amok—is hard for Americans to fathom. The upheaval touched virtually everyone. Chinese dissident and journalist Sasha Gong has a haunting memory of the time. She was a little girl, living with her family in a forty-unit Guangzhou apartment building, when her parents and their neighbors were taken away. "At one point," she recalls, "there was only one adult in the entire building, living among the abandoned children and teens."

During the 1950s and 1960s, China was, to an extent, a silent partner in the Cold War, presenting itself as harmless and backward compared with a superpower like the Soviet Union. While it backed communist forces in the Korean and Vietnam wars, China limited overt expansionist and imperialist dreams to its immediate neighbors. In comparison, the Soviet Union was far more expansionist, deploying troops and military support to various African nations, including Angola, Ethiopia, and Somalia; bolstering Castro's Cuba; and, in fact, providing aid and education to China.

Mao and the CCP's relationship with the USSR was what boxing champion Muhammad Ali might have called an international rope-a-dope. By playing Moscow's poor, distant communist cousin, China exploited the Soviet Union's unsuspecting support, gleaning Russian manufacturing and military secrets while simultaneously weakening its supposed ally and benefactor by receiving monetary and military aid. The USSR was also fighting American active measures on many Cold War fronts at this time. But China's actions helped drain the Eastern Bloc.

The First Move

In 1970, one year after China ominously detonated two hydrogen bombs near its Russian border, Mao sent a message to President Richard Nixon inviting him to visit China. In Washington, this was seen as an intriguing opening. Nixon and his Cold Warrior secretary of state Henry Kissinger saw the opportunity to work with China as a way to further destabilize and isolate the USSR.

Washington policy leaders were completely unaware that China's gambit was a long game. Mao and the CCP—having extracted all they could from the Soviets, who were clearly losing ground to Western technological and economic developments—needed to latch onto a new host.

They found one.

The one with the deepest pockets, the best research and design infrastructure, the most innovative technology, and the strongest armed forces in the world: the United States of America.

In his book *The Hundred-Year Marathon*, China watcher Michael Pillsbury reveals that even as Mao offered his olive branch to Nixon, he regarded the United States as the enemy, and that Chinese documents "likened it to Hitler." Pillsbury also recounts how China's foreign minister, Zhou Enlai, during a meeting with Kissinger, proclaimed that "America is the *ba*." The Chinese interpreter politely rendered this statement as "America is the leader." But this was a blatant mistranslation: "*ba*," as used in most political language, means "tyrant." When the translator was later asked why he softened Zhou's language to Kissinger, he said, "It would have upset him."

It also might have alarmed and enlightened him.

Instead, the United States, unaware of the CCP's hostile attitudes toward it, embraced a policy of helping China in order to destabilize the Soviet Union.

Duplicating its strategy with the USSR, China played the role of the insignificant country. Actually, it didn't have to work very hard at the role, since it was regarded as what the West now calls "a developing nation": extremely poor, with little to no manufacturing technology, limited higher education, and few resources beyond its massive, low-wage workforce. China still claims this status today.

It is easy to see how Nixon, Kissinger, and so many other US leaders were lulled into a false sense of security, despite the CCP's staggering record of human rights abuses and its totalitarian, single-party system. In the 1970s, China's leaders indicated to American diplomats that the country had no problem isolating Russia and ceding more power to the United States on the global stage. The idea of selling American goods to one billion Chinese people somewhere down the line must have been enticing as well.

The Danger of Capitalist Magical Thinking

It is also critical to see how US leaders assumed that building a relationship with China would result in political changes in Beijing. The United States had and still has a vision of itself as a nation builder. We helped reshape Europe after World War II—and did a pretty good job of it. We helped democratize Taiwan. We also helped Japan, South Korea, and, after the end of the Cold War, former members of the Soviet bloc, like Poland and the Czech Republic, grow into democracies.

For some reason, many policy makers and investors seem to assume that capitalism has special powers that can melt away authoritarianism and totalitarianism. History and recent current events, however, tell us this is nothing more than magical thinking.

We have spent billions and billions of dollars trying—and failing—to turn Iraq and Afghanistan into self-sustaining democracies. Egypt, Uganda, and other authoritarian-leaning nations have received billions of dollars in US military and financial aid—and they still can't get over the hump to achieve lasting democracy. Ditto for many of our allies in the Middle East, Africa, and Latin America.

When Deng Xiaoping rose to power in 1978, the CCP recalibrated its attitude toward trade and capitalism. The country was open to receiving foreign investment and participated in the growing global market, but only on its terms. Foreign money could come into China but had to remain there; profits could not be transferred overseas without a great deal of difficulty. China also allowed its citizens to participate in certain Western practices: they could start businesses, create wealth, and wear baseball caps instead of Mao caps. But Beijing kept strict controls over everything else, cementing in no uncertain terms a totalitarian state. There is only one political party with power in China: the CCP. It controls all facets of life in China. It says there shall be no free speech. No freedom of religion. No freedom of the press. The People's Liberation Army is not, in fact, China's army; it is a wing of the CCP. Every business in China must, by law, have a member of the CCP on its board.

In May 1989, there was a brief glimmer of hope that a significant segment of the Chinese population wanted democratic reforms. For three weeks, as many as one million people—students, workers, civil rights leaders—gathered to stage pro-democracy rallies in Beijing's Tiananmen Square. On June 4, the military was called to silence the protesters. A massacre ensued. Reports of the number of protesters slaughtered have varied, ranging from a few hundred, according the CCP, to as many as ten thousand, per a British diplomatic cable. An estimated ten thousand were arrested.

On June 5, one of the most dramatic moments of the late twentieth century occurred: a man holding two shopping bags stood in front of an approaching Chinese tank, blocking its path in a life-or-death game of chicken. The identity of the "tank man" remains a mystery. While millions watched this dramatic showdown all over the globe, to most Chinese citizens, the heroic incident itself remains unknown; images and references to it not only are banned in China but are actively hunted down by sophisticated algorithm-powered censors and thousands of social media monitors.

One month after the Tiananmen crackdown, a telling photo surfaced that was equally disturbing in its way: the sight of US national security adviser Brent Scowcroft and Deng Xiaoping beaming at each other, arms outstretched. Scowcroft was there for a secret meeting at the direction of President George H. W. Bush. That picture and others that surfaced told China and the world everything they needed to know. Bush was backing down. America was willing to concede to China's totalitarian rule. At that point, American foreign policy became about opening markets, and the justification was the belief that free trade would eventually free China. Somehow a theory of the earnings of freedom took hold—an idea that democracy would rule the sleeping giant when per capita income passed $6,000.

James Mann, in his book *The China Fantasy*, calls the West's idea that China will morph into a liberal democratic society "the Soothing Scenario." He summarizes the logic this way: "The country's rapid economic growth will lead to far-reaching political change as well. Eventually, increasing trade and prosperity will bring liberalization and democracy to China."

Mann also talks about the opposite of the Soothing Scenario: "the Upheaval Scenario," in which doubters envision China collapsing as the result of economic chaos or some kind of mass revolution. The result is turmoil and chaos.

Mann was way ahead of the curve when he wrote his book back in 2007—a time when China was literally exploding with commerce and manufacturing. Six years earlier, in 2001, Bill Clinton signed a law passed by Congress establishing permanent normal trade relations with China. With that relationship codified, US investor confidence skyrocketed and so did business. China's economy soared as well, due to a confluence of events: China was then accepted as a member of the World Trade Organization, Apple unveiled the iPod, and an eruption of digital goods turned into an avalanche of international investment.

Despite China's exponential growth, Mann didn't believe in either the Soothing or the Upheaval scenario. For him, all signs indicated that the CCP would continue to hone its brand of authoritarian capitalism. End of story.

And he has been proven absolutely right.

The power of capital and free trade has made China rich. It has lifted hundreds of millions up from poverty. It has also made many investors and business owners outside China untold billions of dollars. But it hasn't made China democratic or increased civil liberties. There is no free press. There is no freedom of speech or religion.

These foundational concepts of the United States and the West are regarded as an existential threat to the CCP—so much so that, in 2013, the party put it in writing. In a position paper known as "Document 9," the CCP states that the promotion of "universal values"—the belief that "Western freedom, democracy, and human rights are universal and eternal"—is an attack on the foundations of the CCP. It goes on to warn against "Promoting Western Constitutional Democracy," which it describes as "an attempt to undermine the current leadership and the socialism with Chinese characteristics system of governance."

Mirror, Mirror

Remember that rope-a-dope move China pulled on the Soviet Union?

They've been using it on America.

While pretending to be battered and struggling, the CCP has weakened America's core strengths: our economy, our technology, our military, our influence on the world stage. But we have allowed this to happen. Our political and economic leaders and our greed helped facilitate this rope-a-dope. We thought we would boost our own wealth, profits, and standard of living. And in a way we have. Stock prices have soared. Real estate markets have boomed, collapsed, and boomed again. But in many ways, we are poorer as a nation. Our infrastructure is a disaster, and many of our cities are plagued by unemployment and drug abuse, victims of the decision to export work to China.

Steve Bannon—Donald Trump's straight-shooting, controversial ex-chief strategist and former Goldman Sachs VP, and US Navy officer—describes the trade-off this way:

> Let's be brutally frank: slaves in China made products financed by London and New York for the unemployed in the West. That's exactly what we've had—slaves in China making products for a neo-feudalist system where the working class and the lower class own nothing and buy cheap shit. They can continue along the hamster wheel because the shit's so cheap because it's provided by slaves and yes, equity values go up. Margins are higher. But it's not a way humans should live.

Bannon is absolutely right. He may be a polarizing figure, but it's worth noting that while hosting a May 15, 2019, CNBC interview with Bannon about Donald Trump's tariff battle with China, liberal globalism champion Thomas Friedman said, "I really agree with so much of what Steve said" about confronting China's unfair trading practices. A year earlier, Friedman had written in *The New York Times* that the president's "instinct is basically right" to hold the line "before China gets too big."

Abandoning manufacturing has been devastating for America. Since the 1970s, US manufacturing plants have shut their doors, lured by the low labor costs of manufacturing in Asia. But for the past twenty years, American businesses have turned China into a manufacturing monolith. We now depend on it for an incalculable number of items, many of which are critical to maintaining our standard of living, such as medical supplies, scientific gear, electronics, and motherboards, as well as the sensors that control our cars, heating systems, and security systems.

So our thirst for profits and our inability to embrace long-term strategies that strengthen our nation have hurt us and helped China. Furthermore, our nation has been gripped by outdated thinking. Most countries, including America, fear that a society will be dramatically changed as a result of a military invasion. But the invasion we are facing is much more insidious. We are slowly having our freedoms eroded by our economic connections to a totalitarian state that openly opposes our core values. Each time a Chinese company invests in a US firm, each time a major American company's data is hacked by the PLA, each time it pays for a congressman or a scientist to attend a junket, each time it opens a Confucius Center on a university campus, the CCP is accruing more influence in the United States.

Our blind generosity has been taken advantage of for nearly fifty years. Since the 1970s, Chinese graduate students have filled out the student body at one US institution of higher learning after another. Many of these students, directed by the CCP and Chinese companies, learned and copied the knowledge of America's world-beating STEM—science, technology, engineering, and math—programs. The funds generated by these students have been used to intimidate and silence scholars within universities who are critical of China.

Since the end of the Cold War, China has failed to commit militarily to war-ravaged places like Syria and Afghanistan but has profited economically while the United States funds the cost of ensuring peace. All those engagements consume US resources. Meanwhile, as laid out in its Belt and Road Initiative—something we'll explore in more depth later—China builds railroads and ports to control the world's shipping supply lines.

The CCP would never agree to an open-ended commitment to rebuild and keep the peace in Afghanistan, where, as of 2018, the Pentagon said it was spending $45 billion per year, with no end in sight. In fact, it is likely the CCP wouldn't even agree to one year of similar expenses.

It is time to delve deeper into China's stealth war, the strategic decisions of Beijing, and our own habit of shooting ourselves in the foot. I aim to lay out the CCP's sophisticated gamesmanship and cold-blooded calculations—as well as the many strategies America and the West can deploy to counter and prevent undue Chinese influence. It will take a sea change to stop the CCP's march, starting with checking our own greed as investors and our own thirst for cheap goods as consumers.

We, as Americans, have a choice. We can sit back and let China weaponize its wealth and influence against us, threatening the great freedoms that are the foundation of our nation. Or we can decide that the business of America cannot be business as usual; our leaders, our entire nation, must recognize the threat we face and combat Chinese influence at every juncture. This is not some alarmist or racist call to action. Let me be clear: I love and admire the Chinese people, their language, and their culture, and when I refer to China, I am almost always referring to the nation controlled by the Chinese Communist Party. It is a thoughtful rebuttal to the influence the Chinese Communist Party has wielded for far too long.

Our fate as the land of the free hangs in the balance.

CHAPTER THREE

ECONOMY

THE STRATEGY OF UNRESTRICTED WARFARE REquires that the battlefield expand.

So the CCP devises and enacts strategies to create influence and power on a global level. But it all starts with a totalitarian force building and wielding economic power, because economic security underpins China's national security. It is the glue that holds China's house of cards together, and that glue—used in tandem with what the authors of *Unrestricted Warfare* call the "bonding agent" of data—has become so strong that what was once a flimsy construction now threatens to become impenetrable.

Every country has a right to compete economically. The problem, however, is that the CCP doesn't believe in straightforward competition. The truth is that China is cheating, and Western US political and corporate leaders, fueled by greed, propaganda, and fear, haven't called it out. That hurts American business and citizens.

In 1991, China had a 2.3 percent share of the world's manufacturing exports. In 2013, it had an 18.8 percent share. The impact of this explosive growth for China has been fairly well documented—the shifts away from agriculture, the migration to cities, the shuttering of state-run enterprises in favor of government-backed free enterprise. But what does this dominance mean for the rest of the world, and specifically for the United States?

For the small percentage of Americans who invest in the stock market, earnings have skyrocketed. For areas of the country where manufacturing was part of the bedrock of the local economy, the loss of this industry has been devastating. Interestingly, among neoclassical economists, the accepted wisdom has been that free trade between two countries improves wealth for both parties. In their 2016 National Bureau of Economic Research (NBER) working paper on the impact of China's manufacturing revolution, "The China Shock," economists David H. Autor, David Dorn, and Gordon H. Hanson say, "Theory assures us that under standard conditions the gains to winners are more than sufficient to offset any losses incurred by those suffering adverse effects from foreign competition." The assumption behind this theory was that displaced workers would be retrained, new industries would arise, wages would not fall, and an equilibrium would be restored at a higher level.

In a 2019 interview, Autor expounded on his paper's findings:

> Economists have long understood two things: One, that free trade among consenting nations increases GDP [gross domestic product] in those countries, allowing them to focus on activities in which they have a comparative advantage. And two, that it's not all-improving, meaning it doesn't make every single person in those countries better off. Even if it expands the pie, it will almost necessarily shrink some slices and grow others. Some people will actually be worse off than they would have been in the absence of trade, even though the country that they live in is wealthier. The second point is where our work was very impactful, showing just how important that second point is. . . . There was a kind of a background assumption that labor markets are fluid. So of course, import competing and manufacturing activities will contract, but people will reallocate quickly into other work.

Over the past twenty years, anyone who has visited the Rust Belt or certain southern districts, which were once the center of American manufacturing, could tell you this assumption is deeply flawed. American manufacturing had been slowing since the end of World War II. The standard of living and the divide between the rich and poor in the United States have exploded since China joined the WTO.

In other words, empirical economists who looked at the data afterward found that economic theory was false: Free trade does not always advance prosperity or lead to a more perfect union.

"The China Shock" offers statistical evidence. From 1990 to 2007, areas "more exposed to increased import competition from China experienced substantially larger reductions in manufacturing employment." Once-active members of the working-age population were unemployed or dropped out of the labor force. Not surprisingly, "US imports from China grew by more than exports—often substantially by more—in nearly every industry," according to the report.

The result? Shock from the dramatic shift in trade: gutted communities, poverty-ravaged cities. In these depleted manufacturing areas, "employment-to-population rates fall at least one-for-one with the decline in manufacturing employment, and generally by slightly more," reports the study.

One other damning study that indirectly showcases the decline of wealth in the United States comes from a distinctly nonpartisan and nonacademic source: the US Census Bureau. Comparing income and property data between the 2000 and 2010 surveys, the bureau's "Distribution of Household Wealth" report found the chasm between America's rich and poor populations expanding at a stunning rate in terms of household net worth (all the assets a household owns minus the debt it owes). The report found that the median households in the bottom 20 percent saw their net worth decrease by $5,124 over the period. Meanwhile, the net worth of the median households in the top 20 percent increased by $61,379.

So the rich got considerably richer and the poor got considerably poorer.

A 2017 study by "The China Shock" trio follows up on the carnage of trade concussions. Its title conveys the intrinsic damage such economic upheaval can cause to a specific sector of the population: "When Work Disappears: Manufacturing Decline and the Falling Marriage-Market Value of Young Men." Here's how the authors summarize what happens in communities where the job market suddenly dries up:

> On average, trade shocks differentially reduce employment and earnings, raise the prevalence of idleness, and elevate premature mortality among young males. . . . Shocks to male relative stature reduce marriage and fertility. Consistent with sociological accounts, these shocks raise the share of mothers who are unwed and share of children living in below-poverty, single-headed households.

These findings are numbing. They point to the vast damage our trade imbalance with China has wrought beyond balance sheets. There seems little doubt that there is a snowball effect in play. The weakening of our job market weakens

American society as a whole, which stresses our economy and security. Less employment leads to less spending and less local tax revenue, which lead to a decline in services and infrastructure, creating a drag on social services. These conditions impact federal spending decisions. A shrinking or unproductive economy taxes available resources. Society as a whole suffers.

Capitalism with Totalitarian Characteristics

In a sense, the CCP has taken its cue from the United States' success. Our country's robust economy has continually aided our growth. America's higher education system, our scientific and technological breakthroughs, our banking system, and our investment instruments have helped build us into a world power. We unshackled competitive forces in the economy while ensuring, by rule of law, that the outcome of those forces aligned with democratic principles. This, combined with our nation's natural resources, created a vibrant, dynamic, innovative, and financially successful nation.

The Chinese Communist Party has basically patterned its structure on this concept—money changes everything—with a number of twists to the formula. It dispensed with rule of law, shed any idea of democracy, and focused all outcomes on the strengthening of a totalitarian state. It aligned private profit motive with the national interest. The totalitarian state of China drives all business with the idea of serving the goals of the CCP. That is the basic tenet.

The party leadership operates from a very focused, tactical, goal-oriented model. It asks, "What do we value? What are our goals? And how do we incentivize our citizens and *the rest of the world* to do the things that we want?" Those italics are there for a reason. Influencing other governments and organizations is the key weapon in unrestricted warfare.

The early leadership of the CCP, like that of the USSR, tried to control production on a granular, individual level, such as dictating worker outputs and which factory would make specific products. But Deng Xiaoping realized that what drives individual initiative is the profit motive. Making money.

Since the CCP controls all monetary policy and access to funds and also controls the legal structure, it puts itself in a position to control all aspects of the economy. It can and does disburse funds. It can and does underwrite entire businesses. It can pass and has passed a law that says every Chinese company must have a CCP committee operating on the premises. It can also banish regulations, and that is just what it has done. On a certain level, the CCP created one of the most laissez-faire (that's French for, basically, "do whatever you want") environments for manufacturing and business. There are no environmental standards. There is no government agency ensuring that products are safe. There is no Better Business Bureau or Bureau of Consumer Protection. The lack of such restrictions and safeguards can make it *seem* as if unbridled, no-holds-barred capitalism has been unleashed. Stealing corporate secrets? Piracy? Theft of intellectual property? Copyright violations? None of these are a problem in China—this is unrestricted warfare applied to global commerce and trade. The fact is, competition among Chinese is often dog-eat-dog—but only as long as the CCP wants it that way.

So that laissez-faire environment that investors and manufacturers love? It can turn on a dime. Because there *is* regulation in China.

Lots of it.

Actually, all of it—since the CCP, by actually choosing not to regulate some sectors, determines what is laissez-faire and what is not.

The fact is, China is a closed economy. Sure, foreign companies can set up shop in China—if they have a Chinese partner, and if that partner has a CCP committee in place to monitor the business. As for foreign investments—once money comes in, it has to stay in China. And when it comes to opening a business in China, like Starbucks or McDonald's, theoretically, at least, all the money it earns must stay in China to either sit in banks or be reinvested. The same rules apply to every company that establishes a business—that is, establishing operations to sell goods or services—in China.

Why is this foreign-investment rule a theory? Because if the right entity applies the right pressure to the CCP, the government will allow some earnings to be sent out of the country. But that is the quiet and reluctant exception, not the rule.

Meanwhile, foreign companies that want to enter the Chinese market—Facebook, YouTube, Twitter, and many others—are banned by the CCP. These sites allow for free expression. They permit posts and videos about religion, oppression in Tibet, the imprisonment of China's Muslim Uighur population, and the beauty of the US Bill of Rights. All those things are forbidden in China, so those companies are not allowed to operate there unless they censor users. This restriction also points to a complete imbalance of trade. China has launched a number of giant, hugely successful knockoffs of Google, YouTube, and Facebook—Baidu, Youku, and Weibo, to name a few. All these sites are available in the United States and around most of the world (where they are monitored by the CCP), but in China, they flourish without American competition.

As for the Chinese unit of money, the yuan? It is not traders on the foreign exchange market who dictate how much it is worth—which is how every other currency in the world is valued—but the Chinese government.

The concept of ownership in China is also fungible. As we'll explore when we delve into China's obsessive acquisition of technology, assets from one company can be transferred to another in the blink of an eye. And if you had a stake in the company that lost those assets, guess what? Too bad. The CCP giveth and the CCP taketh away.

The Free Market Myth

China is predatory and destructive when it comes to the economies of other countries. Countries, in fact, from which Chinese firms generate profits.

Ironically, when critics note that China is not playing fair and make suggestions to force Beijing to play by the same rules everyone else abides by, China apologists launch into a familiar, disingenuous refrain: *That would destroy the free-market system!*

This would be funny if weren't so outrageously hypocritical.

There is no such thing as a free market as long as the second-biggest economy in the world doesn't actually believe in free markets. There is endless evidence that the CCP is dead set against them. There is no free market when a dominant force restricts access, restricts cash flow, and restricts the free flow of ideas.

China invests in an estimated 20 percent of US start-ups as part of its Made in China 2025 plan, unveiled in 2017, which calls for the country to dominate emerging and traditional industries, including new materials, artificial intelligence, integrated circuits, biopharmaceuticals, 5G communications, aircraft manufacture, robots, electric cars, rail equipment, ships, and agricultural machinery. If the plan succeeds, China will not only stop buying from our companies, like Boeing, General Electric, and Intel; it will compete with them in global markets.

Despite this, American investor momentum continues to roll along. In 2019, Morgan Stanley Capital International, a leading index of global stock markets, added a slew of Chinese firms to its coverage. Twenty percent of the index consists of Chinese companies listed on the Shanghai and Shenzhen exchanges. That means that institutional investors and others who use the index as a guide are currently pouring money into those Chinese companies, adding as much as $1 trillion to their valuation within a year.

Given everything we know about China's restrictive monetary policy and cooked-book practices, the fact that so many financial industry leaders are advocating on behalf of a totalitarian juggernaut suggests a number of possibilities: these people aren't paying attention, they are uninformed—which doesn't seem likely, since they all have Bloomberg terminals—or they have been swayed by the profits they've reaped and the insidious propaganda of the CCP, which erroneously portrays the country as a responsible free trade playland.

The other inexplicable refrain many captains of commerce recite is that the free market system is self-regulating. This theory holds that free markets are extremely efficient and that market forces ensure that the business community will always do what's best for itself. This, too, is a false construct and borderline ridiculous. First, as we just demonstrated, with China in the game, there are no free markets. Second, determining the "best" outcome is a dubious proposition—what is best, and for whom? Are quick profits the best result? Or are long-term gains the smarter play? Or is constant liquidity, having convertible cash, what you want? For the past thirty years, the US business community—the investment houses, the Fortune 500 companies, the Securities and Exchange Commission (SEC), pension fund managers—has allied itself in innumerable ways with the CCP, often against its own long-term best interests.

Before we zoom in on the specifics of how the CCP has harnessed its ability to consolidate power in finance, investment, and trade markets to become the most predatory, imperialist economic force on the planet, let's make one more big-picture point about how business, wealth, and prosperity has worked in the United States. It provides a striking contrast to the CCP's machinations.

When Vanderbilt built railroads, when Carnegie built steel mills, when Ford built cars, when Rockefeller dug oil wells, and when IBM built computers, the government didn't back these entities. Banks did. Investors did. The stock market did. As businesses flourished, the economy expanded, technology and housing improved, and the standard of living increased. It was a free market; there was no government plan, although some companies may have received government contracts and tax breaks and some cynical politicians profited from campaign donations and stock tips. And yes, business may have influenced friendly legislation, but business did not serve at the government's beck and call. In fact, things were often the other way around, with governments building roads, water systems, and other infrastructure to allow business to thrive. But government didn't seize what its citizens built; it supported, in essence, a free market.

"China Is a Total Ponzi Scheme"

One of the baffling things about China's rise is how the country has achieved the most mind-boggling growth in the history of the world. There is no other single turnaround like it in modern history. How has it been possible to move so many out of poverty so quickly?

It is a long and complicated story—and one of the subplots of this book—but here is a one-sentence summary from an economic perspective: they did it by issuing and obtaining massive amounts of credit, by generating billions in foreign investment that remains unrecoupable, and by creating a walled, closed economic system that remains unaccountable to outside audits and fleeces foreign investors.

"China's a paper tiger," says Steve Bannon, discussing the country's economic growth. Then the former Goldman Sachs VP told me, "China is a total Ponzi scheme. The only question we have in China, the only important question, is the economic implosion. . . . How bad will it drag down everybody?"

Bannon has a strong case. Imagine if Ponzi scheme king Bernie Madoff, who bilked investors out of billions of dollars for years, had been able—indefinitely—to tell his marks,

"No, you can't take your money out until I say so. And, no, you can only see the financial report that I want you to see." Then imagine if brazen Bernie had been able, also indefinitely, to tell the Department of Justice, the SEC, and the IRS, "No, you can't look at my books. You have to trust my accounting."

If those conditions existed in the United States, Madoff would likely still be fleecing his marks, creating "profits" out of thin air by luring new client cash, taking a cut for himself, and then slowly paying off previous clients.

Those conditions basically describe the rules that China has used to fuel its explosive growth, running a Ponzi scheme on a global scale. Foreign investment comes in, but it stays in China. Some of it remains in dollars so China can continue to trade internationally, but the profits remain in nonconvertible currency and subject to strict capital controls.

Chinese companies, many of which are subsidized by the CCP or used as piggy banks by CCP power brokers, do not follow traditional accounting practices. Therefore, analysts have no way of accurately judging the true fiscal health of Chinese companies, which have a further buffer in that the government-owned Bank of China injects cash into whatever company it deems strategically important. And since, as we'll document in the technology section, the CCP can take assets from one company and instantly assign them to a different company, the idea of regulated bookkeeping is nothing more than a fantasy.

Given all this, the West's rush to invest in China's market

is at best reckless and at worst insane. So why is it happening? Apparently, Wall Street is too high on the profits it reaps on transaction fees for every trade to care. And pension fund managers are too smitten by groupthink investing—the idea that if everyone is doing it, we will, too. They are not alone. The wisdom—or in this case, folly—of crowds is a very powerful force.

To shape that "wisdom," China engages in a form of media warfare: propaganda and influencing campaigns. The CCP's battle to present foreign investment as safe takes place on many fronts. It woos investors and journalists, welcomes trade missions, and sponsors junkets. It buys official-looking advertorial inserts and places them in respected newspapers, such as *The Washington Post.*

China Global Television Network has offered jobs to journalists around the world who have been critical of China's practices, such as deforestation in Africa, in an effort to control the narrative. One reporter, according to *The Guardian*, turned down an offer that would have doubled his salary.

All of this is a part of unrestricted warfare. A calculated charm-and-misinformation offensive designed to build trust and investment.

And let's give the CCP and its propaganda wing credit: they are doing a brilliant job. They are pulling off arguably the biggest con in the world. In November 2018, Chinese president Xi addressed the Spanish Senate, furthering the charade: "China will make efforts to open, even more, its doors to the exterior world, and we will make efforts to streamline access to markets in the areas of investment and protect intellectual property."

He offered no timeline, no details for increased investment access—including whether that alluded to easing divestment rules—and zero on how China would enforce IP protections. It was nothing more than: Trust me.

Part of China's Ponzi success is built on corporate complicity and silence in the West. When companies that have invested heavily in China discover they can't get their money out of the country—and there are literally thousands of these firms out there—what can they do? As soon as they put money in, they find themselves between a rock and a very hard place.

That money is trapped. This is a constant refrain whispered by corporate leaders in high places. According to well-placed finance experts, companies such as Chevron, Exxon, Sony, and BMW have billions of dollars in earnings in China. But they can't repatriate their money. China refuses to let it leave the country, because it needs those dollars. Numerous investment community sources have told me that, as far as they know, China has not allowed the significant repatriation of any Western investor funds since 2015.

"If they're going to grow their economy, they have to grow their reserves, because they have to trade more with the rest of the world based upon that growth," Kyle Bass, the founder of Hayman Capital Management, told me in January 2019. "So China could keep this charade going as long as they maintain the positive current account balance—i.e., more money coming in net than was going out. For the past seventeen years, China generated substantial positive current account balances. Now, for the first time since 2001, they're going to record a negative current account for 2018."

The National Bureau of Statistics of China (NBS) released numbers for 2018 that showed the slowest GDP growth in twenty-eight years, to 6.6 percent. Given the bureau's lack of transparency into the various sectors of China's economy, many financial analysts suspect that these numbers are based on cooked books.

As Bass noted in an editorial a few weeks after the NBS numbers were released, "The last 12 months have seen key Chinese economic indicators such as industrial production, car sales, retail sales and investment all decline to multiyear lows as the previous round of stimulus abated and China's debt burden continued to cause a downward economic spiral."

At any rate, a negative or declining balance—the result of slowing trade and investment—suggests that two fundamentally contradictory things will happen in the short-term: First, China will try to generate more foreign investment to sustain its growth. Second, China will not release any profits on that foreign investment—despite that being the obvious point of investment—because it needs every American cent it can muster to pay for its growth.

If it looks like a Ponzi scheme and acts like a Ponzi scheme but denies it's a Ponzi scheme, what is it?

China.

And the people who invest in it?

They are either coconspirators or victims. Of course, conmen—coconspirators—have other terms for victims. They call them marks.

Or suckers.

ANOTHER DIZZYING DIFFERENCE between China's finance market and Western markets—which again underscores the lack of free trade that exists in Beijing and the manipulative, Ponzi scheme nature of the beast—involves China's habit of selective regulation. In the United States, if IBM issues a bond on the capital markets, that money goes to IBM, and investors should have a good deal of confidence that money raised will be spent to improve the company. After all, there's a board of directors and a CEO who have fiduciary responsibilities to make sure the company hits its goals. In China, incoming investment goes where the CCP wants it to go—again, something we'll examine in greater detail when delving into China's technology obsessions.

Feeding China's Ponzi scheme with American investment creates triple-edged risks, too. The financial industry is not just funding the growth of the United States' number-one totalitarian adversary and risking losing those funds by turning them into nonconvertible capital; it is also drying up valuable investment dollars in the US and other markets. If your pension fund has dollars tied up in China that it can't access, those funds can't be reinvested in rebuilding America's crumbling infrastructure, financing its cutting-edge start-ups, or supporting restarted manufacturing efforts. Wall Street profits may grow—temporarily—but America stagnates.

As the founder of a hedge fund focused on making event-based global investments, Kyle Bass devotes a good deal of time to studying China's balance sheet. He confirms Bannon's take on the subject of China's instability.

In our early January 2019 talk, Bass deconstructed China's numbers and described a closed economic system that is perilously overleveraged in ways that make the United States seem like a bastion of responsible, tightfisted fiscal policy.

Curiously, China's credit strategy runs counter to all the CCP's typical long-term strategy planning, according to Bass. But perhaps this makes sense when you consider that the country has needed quick cash to aggressively implement elements of its long game.

"The way that they've achieved relative stability on their home turf is, they've expanded their central bank balance sheet and printed more yuan than any one country has ever printed currency in the history of man," said Bass.

When Bass compared the fiscal realities that precipitated the 2008 US market collapse to the current state of China's finances, he shuddered.

"Going into the financial crisis," he said, "the US had $17 trillion of GDP and about 1.3 times the GDP in banking assets. And we had about a trillion of banking equity.

When you look at China today, it has a banking system that has 50 trillion dollars' worth of yuan, $2 trillion of banking equity, and an economy (GDP) of $13 trillion."

Bass is basing his numbers on data from the People's Bank of China, the nation's central bank, and other agencies, and he includes such assets as wealth management products, trust beneficiary rights, and trust loans. He estimates China's total credit at $48 trillion, nearly four times its gross domestic product. By comparison, the United States held about $24 trillion in credit in 2019, but its economy was 37 percent larger than China's.

In other words, China had *three times* the amount of money in circulation than the United States did, while generating $4 trillion less in GDP. Even with double the banking equity of the United States—a result of positive returns from 2001 to 2015—those are terrifying ratios. Economic theory and the laws of supply and demand hold that printing massive amounts of money should automatically lead to significant inflation. But so far China has avoided devaluation by refusing to participate in the foreign exchange market. Meanwhile, the CCP controls markets. It also controls the media, ensuring that there will be no stories about shortages or inflation or housing bubbles. And it controls social credit scores—a newly installed system of tracking its citizens' behavior using facial recognition and data surveillance to monitor whether individuals are complying with CCP-mandated laws—which exist as a way to control and reward the population. Together, then, the country's closed economic system and totalitarian repression work to artificially prevent inflation and enforce stability.

Unreal Estate

One telling example of China's market manipulation is how it has coped with a real estate market that many experts believe should be crumbling. Entire ghost cities have been erected, filled with high-rise apartments without a soul in sight. The construction glut has resulted in more than sixty-four million empty apartments, according to estimates. Usually, when there's a surplus of real estate, prices tumble. How has China confounded the laws of supply and demand? "Just by preventing the houses from being sold," explains Bass, noting that an apartment purchased for 100,000 yuan remains on the balance sheet at that price—even if the only offers are for half that much.

The mortgage market is also malleable in the hands of the CCP. "One big reason you're not seeing an immediate property collapse is, they don't really have property tax," says Bass. In the United States, an investor carrying ten vacant apartments would have to pay property tax as well as any payments on a loan. But in China, banks allow people who are behind in a loan just to gross up the loan balance and keep it current. In these instances, it becomes a "rolling loan," explains Bass. "So that if you owe, say, $4,000 on a

$100,000 loan but you don't have the money, the bank will just make your loan balance $104,000, tacking it onto the principal, and say, 'Pay us when you can.'"

Bass says this practice has inspired a saying around his firm: "A rolling loan gathers no loss."

Financing the Future

While the CCP can control the pricing of everything domestically, it is desperately short of resources required to sustain growth. It's one of the largest importers of crude oil in the world, bringing in almost four hundred million tons a year. It imports food, base metals, raw materials, and petrochemicals.

Those dependencies make China's economy extremely vulnerable, according to Bass. As trade slows, as its domestic real estate market implosion looms, as more and more multinational corporations realize they can't repatriate their investments, China's instability grows.

Seen from another perspective, however, this vulnerability also makes the Chinese government dangerous. What steps will the CCP take to ensure it has the cash and the access to foreign capital needed to both sustain itself and continue investing on all the fronts of its unrestricted war? What types of influencing tactics—bribes, blackmail, sabotage, political strong-arming, trade wars—will it resort to in its quest for cash and control?

Pirates, Scams, and Blindness

The story of self-made millionaire A. J. Khubani is the American dream on steroids. But the most recent chapter of his story is the archetypal nightmare that has confronted American manufacturers over the past thirty years. China's flagrant disregard for the international rule of law now threatens the business he built out of nothing.

Khubani's parents immigrated to the United States from India in 1959. Assimilation was family policy. "My family embraced American culture so much, we weren't allowed to speak a foreign language at home," he says.

A.J. was an industrious kid. Growing up in Lincoln Park, New Jersey, he hustled cash by shoveling snow, mowing lawns, and delivering newspapers. He worked his way through state college making pizzas and bartending. By the time he graduated, he had $20,000 in savings. He spent his savings importing a bunch of AM/FM radios, took out an ad in a tabloid, and never looked back.

Long story short, Khubani parlayed his $20,000 into a company—TeleBrands—that designs, develops, patents, and licenses unique consumer products that are frequently sold as part of the As Seen on TV brand. The company has generated more than $1 billion in sales annually for a number of years.

Khubani has a sixth sense for problem-solving products—mini-stairs to help aging and overweight pets get around the house, Big Vision magnifying glasses, digital TV antennae for people who don't want to pay for cable TV—and fun home items like Star Show, which beams laser-light stars onto your house during the holidays. But he also knows how to create a market.

"Our products became popular very quickly," Khubani says, "because of the millions of dollars we spend in advertising. We market them for many years, primarily through television. And then we started selling to retail chains like Walmart, Target, Walgreens. Every major retailer in the country."

In the 1990s, Khubani noticed that his company had become a target of Chinese counterfeiters: "If you went to a flea market, you would find counterfeits of our products. Everything was exactly the same, identical package, identical brand."

His company put in quite a bit of effort locating and shutting down warehouses packed with knockoffs. "It was like a never-ending game of whack-a-mole, where you get rid of one and ten others pop up."

With the rise of the internet, however, the counterfeiting problem grew at an exponential rate. "In 2015, we started noticing counterfeits of our products turning up on Amazon using our trademark, our patented product, using our photographs, using our video, using our copy, using everything."

There were hundreds of listings for bogus As Seen on TV items, and often they were selling for half the Tele-Brands price or lower. Khubani clicked on the low-priced entries and discovered the vast majority of the listings were from sellers in China. No wonder he was seeing his sales figures sagging.

Amazon has two ways of selling products to consumers. One is a traditional retailing arrangement that Amazon calls Vendor Central. The company buys products directly from a vendor, just as any brick-and-mortar store would. The second sales channel is called Amazon Marketplace or, more recently, Seller Central. It is, essentially, a vast digital flea market where anyone with an email account and a bank account can list and sell their goods. Amazon, operating as a middleman similar to eBay, takes a 15 percent commission on every sale.

Based on its page designs, Amazon, evidently, doesn't really care whether it sells a new product via the traditional Vendor sales method or by the Seller method—because it may showcase the Vendor product, but it also showcases links to sellers on the same page, including a display offering items at the lowest price.

But Amazon doesn't monitor each of the millions of listings on its site to see if they are counterfeit. It offloads the responsibility onto the sellers. Here's the company's policy that all sellers must opt into:

> **Representations and Warranties.** You represent and warrant that: (a) Your Services and all aspects of their offer, sale, and performance will comply with all applicable laws, including any applicable licensing, registration, or filing requirements. . . .

When TeleBrands complained to Amazon that thousands of seller listings were illegal, Khubani says his company was told, "We have no way of verifying that these are illegal items. You need to clean up your own marketplace. It's not our responsibility to check if sellers are listing counterfeits. You need to go after these counterfeiters yourself."

Infuriated, Khubani's team asked for the names and contact information of the sellers listing counterfeit goods, so that they could pursue them. They were told: "That's against our policy. We can't identify them."

As frustrating as that exchange was, two other realities left Khubani feeling even more enraged and powerless. The first was that even if he could identify the sellers, he had no legal recourse in China—the government there has made it clear for three decades that it will not stop counterfeit goods from being made or exported. But the second involved Amazon and the US government.

Amazon is a terrific logistics company. It has to be; efficiency adds to its bottom line. If it can't move products quickly at the lowest possible cost, its profits will shrink. So it seeks to optimize shipping for itself and its sellers to provide a great experience for its customers. One way it does this is with a service called Fulfillment by Amazon. Sellers ship their goods to Amazon fulfillment centers and pay for storage and per-item fulfillment. Amazon has opened a number of fulfillment centers in China. As far as Khubani was concerned, the existence of these centers meant that Amazon was basically making it easier for pirated and counterfeit goods—based on products in which he had invested hundreds of millions of dollars developing, patenting, and marketing—to reach consumers and destroy his business.

"Everyone thinks Amazon is this great American company," says Khubani, who notes that Amazon did start removing bogus sellers after New Jersey senator Cory Booker made a call on his behalf. "But part of the reason they are making money is that they are aiding and abetting the sale of counterfeit products. And nobody knows this."

But Amazon wasn't the only one making it easy for these predatory pirates to thrive. A willing, perhaps unwitting partner made shipping these illegal goods from China incredibly cost efficient: the US Postal Service. The Universal Postal Union (UPU), established in 1874, sets mail delivery fees for national carriers in 192 countries. Under a 1969 provision to help struggling economies, the US Postal Service agreed to offer a huge discount for packages shipping out of China that weigh less than 4.4 pounds. How big a discount? Big enough that the postal service says it is losing $170 million a year on the deal.

An example: it costs more to ship a three-pound package on a 2.3-mile journey from 1600 Pennsylvania Avenue in Washington, DC, to the US Capitol than it does to ship the same item 6,925 miles from Beijing to the White House.

Khubani was aghast. The US government was subsidizing shipments of illegal goods that were eroding his company's profits and threatening its stability. And there was nothing he could do about it.

"Every other manufacturer I speak to that makes consumer products is facing this huge issue," he says.

And it is more than just an Amazon problem. Yair Reiner is the Brooklyn-based inventor of the Frywall stovetop splatter guard—a colorful silicone cylinder designed to be set inside a frying pan to keep sizzling, bubbling grease and fat from flying all over the place. Sales of the product exploded after Reiner appeared on the *Today* show and wowed the stars of *Shark Tank*, where his Frywall demo sparked a bidding war among the show's entrepreneurs. With success, though, came the counterfeiting from China.

Bootleggers on Amazon have been the least of Reiner's problems. In fact, he has made it clear that Amazon is his company's most profitable channel by far. But Chinese-manufacture knockoffs of the Frywall—billed as Frywalls—have been showing up all over the internet—on Google search results, on eBay, on individual websites created specifically to sell these fakes.

"There's all kinds of infrastructure, some in the US and other Western countries and some of it based in China, that facilitates the manufacturing, marketing, and distribution of knockoff products," says Reiner, a former equity research managing director at Oppenheimer & Co.

But Reiner's nightmare begins in China, where manufacturers place fake Frywalls on Alibaba, the massive e-commerce site that allows bulk orders—think of it as eBay for retailers—and on AliExpress, which operates like Amazon's Marketplace and offers single orders from a variety of sellers. These items typically list for 25 percent less than what Reiner charges for a real Frywall.

AliExpress is a hugely popular online shopping destination in China and many other markets. But it remains comparatively unknown in the United States. So selling these illegal products to stateside consumers is where Amazon, eBay, and individual websites come into play.

"Essentially, these resellers are advertising a product without ever taking possession of it and actually holding inventory," Reiner says. "When they receive an order from Amazon, eBay, or a web store they've created that also offers hundreds of other 'vapor' products, they route it to AliExpress vendors and have it sent directly from China to the consumer in the United States. And they can do this seamlessly, because there are tools that allow them to basically link their eBay or Amazon listing or a site created with Shopify straight to an AliExpress vendor."

While Reiner believes many of the listings are created by the Chinese manufacturer, the reality is that anyone anywhere in the world can create a listing and make a sale without ever taking possession of the illegal Chinese-made product and without laying out a dime for inventory.

And if the order is shipped to the United States from China, the 1969 UPU agreement ensures the cost of delivery will be cheaper than anything Reiner can offer from his Brooklyn office. He believes ending the shipping subsidy would stop the losses to his web sales—no one would pay $15 or $20 to ship an item from China when it ships for $3.99 in the United States.

As for smuggling in illegal bootleg Frywalls, Reiner sees that as less of a problem. The web sellers' business model, he says, "is to do all of this without actually taking on any inventory risk. Shipping counterfeit product in bulk would increase the risk. First, you've got to bring it here, and then hope you sell it without getting caught and having your bootlegs seized."

Reiner estimates that he and his head of marketing spend about 5 percent of the week policing bogus listings and contacting Amazon, eBay, and Shopify to remove them, plus thousands of dollars consulting lawyers. "There's a kind of spiritual cost to this, too," he says. "We're a very small operation, and we feel we're constantly fighting this uphill battle. We're trying to fight the good fight and innovate and create a great product and delight customers and stand behind everything that we do. But with everything we do building the company and the product, we're subsidizing these predatory fuckers. So it's hard to stay level and centered. Which is why ending the subsidy would be a huge step in the right direction."

The Ship Slip

Approximately two hundred million shipping containers moved through Chinese ports in 2017, according to the *Journal of Commerce*. The most commonly used container, a twenty-foot equivalent unit (TEU), is twenty by eight by eight feet, with an internal capacity of 1,170 cubic feet and a maximum weight of 67,196 pounds. Giant freighters like the New-Panamax and the truly massive Ultra Large Container Ship—vessels so big they cannot dock at most US ports—hold 14,000 and 20,000 TEUs, respectively. The logistics of shipping every imaginable product on earth—from toys, salt, and bananas to nuclear reactors, oil, and mousetraps—have been standardized by the International Organization for Standardization (ISO), which works with more than 160 countries to codify the acceptable sizes of containers to make loading and unloading goods as uniform and efficient as possible.

The ISO 9001 is the international standard for a quality management system for shipping compliance. Being ISO 9001 certified means that a company follows the standard's guidelines, fulfills its own requirements, meets statutory and regulatory requirements, and maintains documentation. Companies are granted certification in different aspects of business—engineering, manufacturing, and so on—after the successful completion of a registrar's audit. Certification supposedly confers legitimacy on a company: its products are safe, stable, and won't break when you open them.

An estimated twelve million TEUs are shipped from China to the United States each year, which breaks down to nearly 33,000 containers per day. The United States is allowed four—4!—shipping inspectors in China. That means each inspector would have to inspect roughly 8,250 US-bound containers a day. But of course that would be impossible, considering there are at least twenty ports in China used for international shipping and none of these four inspectors can be in five places at once.

Even if China allowed the United States to have twenty or two thousand shipping inspectors, these containers would not be vetted in any meaningful way, because the inspectors are not allowed to actually inspect the containers. All they can do is look at the manifests—that is, they look at a list of what companies say is in the container. A container could be stocked with two hundred pairs of socks lying on top of five thousand pounds of fentanyl, but if the manifest says "20,000 pairs of white athletic socks" are being shipped by a company with ISO 9001 certification, there is no need to check. The container is loaded and delivered.

The ISO 9001 should be regarded as a largely meaningless rubber stamp certification in China, not a confidence-inspiring designation of quality assurance. The company that administers 50 percent of the audits and certifies the results is owned by the CCP, and the CCP has no interest in slowing down production, sales, or exports that could bring in dollars. Furthermore, the auditors are easily bribed.

As for the Chinese inspectors who work the ports, being

vigilant and busting shipments containing illegal goods or products not listed on the manifest are frowned upon. Opening up a container and searching it takes time. And time is money. Delaying the loading and departure of a ship is the kind of thing inspectors can get fined for.

So this is how and why American markets have been flooded with counterfeit goods. There are no checks and balances in China ensuring quality control. There is no Consumer Protection Agency, no Environmental Protection Agency, Patent or Trademark Office, no FDA or IRS, no one is interested in ensuring that products are not harmful and that there is copyright protection, culpability, and good governance. If tires explode, if airbags don't open, if a brake-pad sensor fails after one hundred miles, if a licensing fee wasn't obtained, if a product contained a poison, so what? The products are gone. The sale is made. Next!

Corporate Espionage 2.0

Corporate espionage and intellectual property (IP) theft rarely get talked about.

If a jewelry store or a museum is robbed, the cops are called. The newspapers report on the heist and talk about the value of what was stolen. It becomes a quantifiable event—"a $2 million haul" or a "$10 million painting." Everyone talks about the crime at work, on Twitter, on late-night TV. When suspects are identified, a manhunt ensues.

But with corporate espionage and IP theft, there is usually a cone of silence. Done well, corporate theft is invisible. It involves copying documents, engineering plans, chemical formulas, computer codes, raw data. That's different from stealing a Picasso off a museum wall. Imagine stealing the painting and replacing it with an excellent forgery, though, one so good that it takes a whole year for an expert to notice the original has vanished. This kind of delayed "we've been robbed" reaction happens all too often in the corporate world, but the reaction is muted. Reporting the theft can lower investor confidence, hurt company morale, and tip off competitors.

A number of well-known auditing and accounting companies—Ernst & Young, Deloitte, PricewaterhouseCoopers, KPMG—conduct private investigations into suspected corporate espionage. The level of CCP-sponsored attacks these firms encounter varies from the most basic—bribing employees to copy documents, placing students at research institutes and pressuring them to steal—to sophisticated, multioperative hacking raids and full-blown intelligence operations.

In 2014, the chairman of a large hedge fund sent me a privately commissioned briefing about illicit Chinese activity in US corporations. The briefing was stunning in scope and detail. And the information it contained shook my view of the world to its very foundations.

The most disturbing slides detailed an assault to gain control of a proprietary technology that a fledgling firm had developed. The method of attack reminded me of the sophistication of an air campaign. It was perfectly choreographed to create subtle misdirection and open up a target for a blitzkrieg. The operation highlights the enormous amount of resources the CCP will dedicate to sabotaging corporate rivals to obtain control over coveted technology. Here's what happened.

An American chemical company, owned by a private equity firm, had patented some groundbreaking green technology and was growing at a steady clip. Its owner began developing a five-year plan to take the company public.

But suddenly, the company started missing its earnings targets. The problems appeared to be in sales—orders were down—and in logistics, the division that handled the flow of products. The sales guy was fired, but the bleeding continued. The owners met with the leadership team and warned them to fix the issues, because continued shortfalls would put the planned IPO in jeopardy. Not long after that, the company received an unsolicited offer from a Chinese company. The offer shocked the owners—it was 30 percent below what the value should have been, had it not been for the shortfalls. Management was stunned: How did these suitors make such an accurate valuation without company data? It seemed like they knew about the recent losses.

The owners hired investigators. They discovered that not only had the chemical company been hacked, but so had the private equity firm that owned it. The hackers knew the company's earnings targets and red lines in terms of what was unacceptable to the owners.

The level of sabotage was, on a spy craft level, brilliant. The email servers were selectively hacked, so that when the company would send out solicitations for orders, hackers would delete them before they were sent. Similarly, when orders came in, some of them never made it into the sales team's inbox—because the hackers pulled them out. The selective sabotage was enough to hurt sales but not enough to trigger an investigation.

Meanwhile, the hackers also damaged back-end logistics. When an order came in for, say, a thousand units, hackers would change the number to nine hundred. When the shortfall was discovered—usually after the order was shipped or about to be shipped—a backorder would be created. This subtle move created added costs for labor, delivery, and other sectors, which impacted the bottom line.

It was a dazzling operation. Subtle, almost imperceptible. The only entity that would have the resources and sophistication to execute such an elaborate ruse would be the state.

This sinister operation crystallizes the level of economic warfare that China was engaged in. It wasn't just stealing—copying documents is the corporate equivalent of a smash-and-grab robbery. This was a strategic sting on a number of levels. At some point, the CCP had set industrial policy and made green technology a priority. Once the American chemical start-up was identified, someone spearheaded an operation that required both intelligence planning, hacking by the People's Liberation Army, and oversight and analysis by a Chinese-owned business. The goal was to sabotage and devalue an American company in order to acquire it at a below-market price, to obtain technology that the CCP considered vital. It was nothing less than a government-sanctioned assault on an American company.

When I joined the Joint Chiefs of Staff, in 2014, I shared this brief with practically everyone I met in the Pentagon. The reaction was always the same: "Oh my God, this is horrible!" Then they'd say, "That's not my job." And of course, in keeping with the military's traditional mission, that made perfect sense. The job of the military is to plan the fight, prepare for the fight, execute the fight, or maintain order. Protecting American businesses? That's nothing to do with us!

But to me, this was a clear-cut act of war. It was hostile; it was predatory; it was in violation of international law. And it was meant to hurt our nation.

I went to the Treasury and the Department of Commerce. I met with the State Department. The response I got was jaw-dropping: "China's not our adversary, they're our friends" was the standard response. "We cooperate with them." I would look at them and think, "But I just *showed* you research *that proves they are not our friends.*"

I came to the conclusion that there was nobody doing anything about China's trade espionage and economic warfare. It was a hot potato issue, and nobody wanted to touch it. I finally found one ally in the Joint Chiefs of Staff. I don't want to name him, but I regard him as a hero. Unlike so many senior officers, he understood that economic warfare was, in fact, warfare and that the military has a duty to protect new frontiers. And he gave me the go-ahead to study Chinese economic hostilities and develop strategies to address issues.

When I told people what I was working on, a frequent response would come in the form of a disbelieving question: "Why are you looking at this?"

My answer: "Because nobody else is."

Trade Market Mayhem

Sabotage and espionage are just two ways to upend a market. The CCP also relies on many other strategies to control and dominate markets, from predatory pricing and bait-and-switch deals to old-fashioned bullying.

Let's start with bullying. China is the world's leading producer of seafood, generating nearly seventy million tons in 2017. It employs an estimated one million people in its frozen fish industry, which is also the largest in the world. China's seafood exports totaled $19.3 billion in 2016.

Interestingly, wild fish caught within Chinese ocean waters during the first nine months of 2017 declined 11.9 percent, but according to the US Department of Agriculture, fish caught in other territorial ocean waters increased by 14.2 percent from the previous year.

In other words, China, which accounts for more than

60 percent of global production of cultured seafood, can't sustain its wild seafood production by relying on catches from its own coastal waters. So what does it do? It sends its fishing vessels around the world to raid the coastal waters of weaker states, frequently preying on nations that don't have strong or even any naval forces.

To be clear, fishing in international waters is perfectly legal. But exploiting the riches of, say, Ecuador's Galapagos Islands—where, in August 2017, twenty Chinese fishermen were found with a catch of 6,600 sharks—is a violation of international law. According to the United Nations Convention on the Law of the Sea, exclusive economic zones for fishing extend two hundred nautical miles from a national coastline.

In South America, Chinese ships have been spotted fishing in the waters of Argentina, Chile, Peru, and other nations. In March 2016, the Argentine coast guard caught a Chinese ship, the *Lu Yan Yuan Yu*, fishing in its waters and fired a warning shot to stop it. The *Lu Yan Yuan Yu* tried a ramming maneuver, but it backfired; the Argentineans fired, and the ship sank. Today, many Chinese fishing vessels outfit themselves with buffers that can serve as battering rams and prevent other ships from closing in on them.

While China claims it is monitoring the situation aggressively, Chinese trawlers have nevertheless been spotted as far away as South Africa.

Strong-arming smaller nations in order to steal their natural resources is one tactic. Offering generous development deals that mask usurious terms is another. China is currently in the midst of building out its multitrillion-dollar Belt and Road global infrastructure initiative to dominate the delivery of goods across the planet. We'll dive deeper into the implications and intent of Belt and Road later on, but since we're discussing market control, it's worth noting two things: that controlling shipping is one method of creating a stranglehold on trade flows, and that building out infrastructure for economically challenged countries is a great way to gain economic leverage in the countries you are supposedly "helping." These initiatives are, in a sense, debt and market-access traps.

One recent example of how China manipulates "helpful foreign aid" into "control" is the massive Hambantota Port project in Sri Lanka, a war-torn country that has not been high on anyone's list of trading partners for decades. But over the ten-year period during which Sri Lanka president Mahinda Rajapaksa held office, the state-owned China Harbor Engineering Company struck enormous deals for cash and credit to build the multibillion-dollar deep-dredged port on the southern end of the island.

Rajapaksa lost the presidential election in 2015, leaving the new leaders swamped by the debt of his China deals. And China, acting more like a loan shark than a benevolent ally, refused to ease up on negotiated terms. In 2017, the Sri Lankan government handed over control of the port and fifteen thousand acres of land around it for ninety-nine years.

China now has a port that both abuts and skirts India, its largest manufacturing competitor. And while the lease for Hambantota prohibits China from using it for naval purposes, there is considerable concern that it will try to negotiate those terms or, as it so often does with legal matters, just ignore them.

For all intents and purposes, however, it is clear that China didn't exactly "help" Sri Lanka improve its infrastructure—it swamped the country in debt and has now gained significant economic control over the struggling but strategically placed nation.

Giving sweetheart deals to nations with stagnating economies is actually standard operating procedure for certain CCP-backed companies. And the strings that are attached may not always be evident. China has been extremely active in Africa. In 2018, President Xi pledged $60 billion to $80 billion in aid to African nations. "China does not interfere in Africa's internal affairs and does not impose its own will on Africa," Xi said. "What we value is the sharing of development experience and the support we can offer to Africa's national rejuvenation and prosperity."

But accepting Chinese money is fraught with issues. If China builds out a phone network, it owns the IP. If a Chinese company builds a power plant, it owns the plans and the operation. And these projects, like Sri Lanka's port, can be debt traps. Controlling vital infrastructure allows China to apply pressure in other areas. Reports note that African governments have been pressured not to recognize Taiwan. No doubt they will be pressured to remain silent on China's repression of Uighurs, Tibet, and free speech advocates. In this way, aid money can be turned into what might be termed a freedom trap.

In a remarkably short time, Transsion Holdings, a Shenzhen company founded in 2006, has captured the African mobile phone market and unseated Korean global giant Samsung. The newcomer devised some Africa-specific innovations, like multiple SIM card slots, allowing the phone to be shared among users with different numbers and service providers. Models were designed to have longer battery life, given that electricity is a rare commodity in parts of the continent. But the company acquired customers by undercutting the market on pricing, reportedly offering the phone for as little as $50.

Transsion Holdings, then, has succeeded through innovation and aggressive pricing. Was that pricing underwritten by the Bank of China? Who knows? Should these new customers feel comfortable about the privacy of their data? They have reason to be nervous. With most Chinese enterprises, the risk of CCP interference is always a possibility. As noted earlier, every Chinese corporation must have a CCP member on its board. And an African country dominated by Transsion—or any country that relies on Chinese telecommunications—may one day run the risk of its data being abused for economic purposes or to maintain social control.

Down on the Corner

"Rare-earth metals" sounds like the name of a progressive rock band. And the specific names of these elements—dysprosium, neodymium, gadolinium, and ytterbium—sound like planets on *Star Trek*. But they are among the most important materials in our digital era, used in key components in the manufacture of everything from smartphones and hard drives to radar and advanced weapons systems.

Legend has it that Deng Xiaoping once said, "There is oil in the Middle East, but there are rare earths in China." The fact is, there are rare-earth metals in other places—including California, which once hosted a giant mine owned by the now-defunct Molycorp—but when China became a low-cost supplier, it pushed everyone else out of the market.

As of 2019, China owns an estimated 90 to 95 percent of the supply of these metals. This gives it the ability to stop electronics manufacturing anywhere in the world. All the CCP has to do is decide to restrict exports, or it could set prices so high that the cost prohibits purchase.

It's a scary prospect. But not as scary, perhaps, as other markets China has cornered. It is the world's number-one producer of cement, steel, and chemical fertilizer. There are plenty of stunning metrics that convey China's otherworldly growth, but the claim that the country used more cement between 2011 and 2013 than the United States consumed in the entire twentieth century may be the most jaw-dropping. It simply doesn't seem possible. And yet it makes perfect sense: as of 2015, China produced about 80 percent of the world's air conditioners, 70 percent of its mobile phones, and 60 percent of its shoes, according to the *Economist.* To make all that stuff, you need a lot of concrete to build factories.

CHAPTER FOUR

THE MILITARY CRISIS

FOR AS LONG AS MOST READERS WILL REMEMBER, the United States has maintained a considerable military advantage over any potential rivals on the planet.

This is no longer the case.

As a former career officer in the US Air Force, it hurts to write those words. But the US military needs a reality check, and has needed one for the past two decades.

We achieved military dominance largely as a result of President Ronald Reagan's "peace through strength" policies, spending more money on weapons, equipment, and armed forces than any other nation. While spending levels have continued to remain relatively high, our political and military leaders have been slow to realize that China has been fighting a strategic war for decades. This lack of understanding has resulted in ceding gains—strategic, geographical, technological, and digital—to the People's Liberation Army.

Take these together, factor in our abandonment of military research and development expenditures and all our costly deployments around the globe starting in the 1990s, and you've just written the equation for the erosion of US military superiority.

When it comes to deployment, the US military aspires to be nimble and reactive. In many ways, we are still the best in the world at moving military forces and reacting to global emergencies. But the entrenched business-as-usual priorities of the military-industrial complex—with its focus on short-term hardware procurement and raw military might at the expense of R&D, long-term planning, and rethinking the defense industrial base—have hindered our ability to adjust, to recalibrate and strategize accordingly. Senior leaders at the Pentagon need to recognize that the modern battlefield includes 1s and 0s and dollars and cents. Where is our equivalent cyber force to protect America's data? Where is our office for economic warfare or for counterpropaganda?

In no way do I mean to denigrate our armed forces. I seek to improve them. Since the collapse of the Soviet Union, America has assumed a role as the world's policeman, and our forces have ensured stability, ended wars, and promoted peace in Africa, Europe, and the Middle East. We have also entered two decades-long military engagements in Afghanistan and Iraq. These wars have proven extremely costly, and we have shouldered far more than our share of the expense—it is an unassailable fact that many of our NATO allies have not adhered to agreed-upon contributions. The wars take up personnel, equipment, and billions of dollars; bog down our military; and prevent the Pentagon from making needed investments in R&D, social cyber warfare, and the type of weapons systems that China cannot defend against.

And while our military has been taking fire, battling the Taliban, Al Qaeda, and ISIS, the Chinese have been busy waging their quiet noncombat war: assembling an enormous cyber division; obtaining sophisticated weapons technology; constructing ports, islands, and military bases; installing telecom technology—a key tool for spy craft—and using American investment to build its defense systems.

Reality Check

The United States cannot fight a ground war without China.

Well, we could. For a little while. But the amount of goods and materials that have shipped and continue to ship from China for military use is mind-boggling. Yes, there are laws mandating that the US military buy goods that are made in America, but a daunting amount of military equipment contains components made in China. The propellant that fires our Hellfire missiles, which are launched from helicopters, jets, and drones, is imported from China. The glass in night-vision goggles contains a metal called lanthanum, the vast majority of which comes from China. Our officers write plans and reports and print them out on computers, which come predominantly from China. Instructional videos are watched on screens made in China. The handheld video game players that entertain off-duty troops? Largely made in China.

The list goes on and on. It's absurd.

If supply lines were cut from China, if a trade war broke out with embargoes, the US military would have a nightmare sourcing its needs and getting them to the battleground, wherever that might be.

Ironically, the way we would communicate about these shortages also relies on China: we don't manufacture any mobile phones in this country. The army uses phones. Lots of them.

"Our almost complete dependence on China and other countries for telecommunications equipment presents potentially catastrophic battlefield vulnerabilities," wrote Brig. Gen. John Adams, US Army, retired, in a 2015 essay.

This is a daunting concept. We've outsourced ourselves to a point where we can't defend ourselves and our interests without Chinese manufacturing and logistical support.

Fortunately, at the moment, China has no interest in engaging in a ground war or any kind of war that entails actual violence and physical destruction. It does, however, have an interest in supplying goods for wars. The CCP would rather boost its coffers servicing our troops and use that revenue to bolster its strategic positions, build out its Belt and Road infrastructure plan—which will eventually create the global footprint and supply chain for its own army, "should" the need arise—and invest in high-tech weapons to fuel that army.

Indeed, using Western capital, never mind Western technology, to build its military is part of the CCP strategy. "Between January 2004 and January 2015," Gabe Collins reported in the *Diplomat*, "the publicly listed arm of China Shipbuilding Industry Corporation, CSIC Limited, and that of China State Shipbuilding Corporation, CSSC Holdings, raised a combined total of $22.26 billion from selling stock and bonds."

"Every dollar . . . raised on the market and ploughed into upgraded yard infrastructure, staff, and warship equipment frees up military budget funds for other uses," Collins astutely notes. It's worth adding that the Chinese Navy has outstripped our American fleet in sheer numbers. As of 2017, China's navy had 317 ships; the US Navy had 287.

We'll return to discussing the rival naval forces in a moment, but first let's examine one effort to fund a tangential part of the China war machine that backfired. It shows both how China tries to lure foreign investment against the West's interests and how compliance to international standards of fair trade can stop Chinese manipulation in its tracks.

On July 2, 2015, the Stock Exchange of Hong Kong published documents revealing that the China Communications Construction Company (CCCC), the largest port-dredging company in the world, had filed plans to spin off a subsidiary, CCCC Dredging, in an IPO targeted to raise from $800 million to $1 billion.

Numerous reports have named CCCC as the company that built the controversial man-made islands in the Spratlys archipelago in the South China Seas. These islands are viewed by many in the international community as illegal constructions, built for the purposes of housing aggressive military installations and furthering China's dubious claim to policing international waters. One of the islands, Fiery Cross Reef, home to a three-kilometer runway and missile and radar installations, was built by CCCC at an estimated cost of $11 billion.

CCCC's role in the creation of the islands and military installations was a huge red flag for some market watchers. One of them was Roger Robinson. His global risk consulting firm, RWR Advisory Group, obtained the prospectus for the IPO. Nowhere in the document did CCCC mention its island-building in the South China Sea. Since CCCC reportedly built the islands, and in light of the international censure, the company faced a strong possibility of legal exposure. Furthermore, The South China Sea and East China Sea Sanctions Act, introduced by Florida senator Marco Rubio in 2017 and still under consideration, would target "any Chinese person that contributes to construction or development projects in areas of the South China Sea contested by one or more members of the Association of Southeast Asian Nations (ASEAN)," and would render CCCC as a potential sanctionable entity because of its role.

Robinson's team contacted the Hong Kong exchange and asked whether the CCCC admitted to island-building in any documents. The answer was no.

"We basically made the point that there's a material risk that the company could be sanctioned, and that clearly represented a material risk to prospective shareholders," Robinson explained.

The stock exchange representatives went back to CCCC Dredging and directed it to update its prospectus. The company refused, insisting there was nothing controversial.

"They said, 'We're not going to dignify this notion that this territory is disputed. This is our sovereign territory. It's no different than Exxon drilling off of New Jersey,'" said Robinson. "They actually used that argument!"

Robinson's team then warned the Hong Kong exchange that it was exposing itself to legal action if it sponsored the IPO, because it had prior knowledge of risk. A class action suit against the exchange would be sure to follow.

"Finally, the Hong Kong exchange went back to CCCC and said, 'No, we have to insist,'" said Robinson. "And CCCC Dredging pulled the IPO and walked away. That's a billion dollars in forgone money. The IPO is, to my knowledge, the only price that China has ever paid for its illegal island-building in the South China Sea after all this time."

Sunken Defenses

Let's return to the issue of naval superiority. The big selling point for analysts who insist that the US Navy has bigger, better ships than China is the fact that US aircraft carriers outnumber, outperform, and dwarf China's. Given that differential, it's easy to see how people might assume this gives the United States a huge advantage.

That assumption, however, would be wrong.

China's geographic location and its missile capability provide it with a very comfortable defensive cocoon. The two countries are thousands of miles apart. And while the United States has military installations in Japan and South Korea, and the daunting flexibility of those aircraft carriers, China has created defenses that nullify the power of those forces.

China has thousands of precision warheads tied to a sophisticated command and control system. Its Dong Feng–26 ballistic missile—46 feet long, 44,000 pounds, and built to carry both nuclear and conventional warheads—was designed to obliterate aircraft carriers. The DF-26 has a range of 2,500 miles, which means it can strike US warships in the western Pacific Ocean, including ships based in Japan. So do the math: in order to deploy a carrier's bombers on a mission in the South China Sea, the carrier would have to come within range of DF-26 and other missiles that would destroy it. And while the US Navy has SM-6 interceptor missiles, thought to be capable of destroying a DF-26, the sheer amount of smaller, long-range ballistic missiles at China's disposal and the blazing speed with which these weapons travel (six thousand miles in thirty minutes) pose, at the moment, an enormous threat to our ships. It is conceivable that an undetected conflict might end in thirty seconds. Game over.

Looked at from an economic standpoint, the PLA constructed a $1 billion missile system designed to destroy a $30 billion ship. There is no doubt our carriers are valuable and powerful machines. But their effectiveness in policing the Pacific is now extremely limited.

While China has made great strides in missile deployment, US armed forces have been unable to match production because of the 1987 Intermediate-Range Nuclear Forces Treaty between the United States and the Soviet Union. This pact not only called for both parties to stop building nuclear and conventional ground-launched ballistic and cruise missiles with ranges of 500 to 5,500 kilometers; it also called for the elimination of these weapons. By 1991, 2,692 weapons had been destroyed.

In other words, after the United States began emptying its silos in the hopes of reducing danger and destruction, China, which was not part of the treaty, began acquiring the technology to build and then stockpile an enormous arsenal.

Meanwhile, the Russian government eventually stopped

adhering to the treaty. In February of 2019, after repeatedly warning Russia about illegal missile deployments near Ukraine, the United States announced that it was ending the treaty—effectively setting a path toward answering China's missile threat.

Lest anyone think I'm picking on the Navy, my own department, the Air Force, has slipped, too. Our most impressive fighting machine, the F-35, has also been stripped of its power by Chinese technology, and I'll explain why soon.

China has also built a very sophisticated command and control network, known as the C4ISR (Command, Control, Communications, Computers, Intelligence, Surveillance, and Reconnaissance), in the Pacific. This network uses technology (computers) to sync the military's operational decision-making (command and control) with the ability to synthesize and analyze the military information (intelligence, surveillance, and reconnaissance) quickly and initiate (communications) offensive and defensive actions. Think of C4ISR as the most sophisticated alarm and response system on the planet—one that creates operational and strategic advantages by using land-based radar, remote sensors, manned and unmanned military platforms, and intelligence data to optimize outcomes on the battlefield.

The US armed forces do not have a fully operational C4ISR equivalent in the Pacific, but we need one, because right now our command and control capabilities there rely heavily on satellites. If these satellites were attacked and disabled, our ability to use some of our most deadly instruments of deterrence would be critically impacted. So now, more than ever, we need to have a totally secure second network to ensure that our systems are safe and running at maximum efficiency.

The foundation of that second network is something called 5G.

Don't forget that term. Our nation's security depends on it.

Remember those aircraft carriers we were talking about? They are powered by nuclear reactors. Once I became aware of China's strategy, I began to think differently about the policies that the Department of Defense should be concerned about.

Friendly Fire

In the winter of 2015, while I was working for the Joint Chiefs of Staff, I received an email notifying me that the United States was going to sign the renewal of something called a 123 Agreement with China. I had never heard of this type of agreement, so I made some inquiries and got ahold of the proposal.

The 123 Agreements are named after section 123 of the Atomic Energy Act of 1954, which is basically an agreement of cooperation in order to share peaceful nuclear technology with foreign countries. So far, we have these agreements in place with more than forty countries.

I thought about the ramifications of this for about five seconds and reached a clear and present conclusion: signing the proposed 123 Agreement with China was a terrible idea. There were many reasons for this determination.

The proposed agreement would allow China to buy the Westinghouse AP1000 nuclear power plant. Yes, the reactors in these power plants are built and sold to generate safe energy—which many nations need. I instantly realized that the Chinese would now have reactors and would quickly reverse engineer the process so they could figure out how to build their own reactors, since no technology, once deployed in China, is safe from being pirated.

But allowing China to steal and manufacture power plants—while anticompetitive, illegal, and corrupt—wasn't my biggest concern.

Not even close.

Selling this technology to China meant that the know-how that went into their development would aid the PLA in improving their own naval nuclear reactors. By agreeing to this deal, we would be sharing engineering expertise that could be used against us in a hostile manner—with a nation that has openly declared its hostility.

There was no way we could let this happen. It was as if we would be giving away national security secrets.

I sent a message back: "The Joint Staff absolutely does not agree with renewing this deal."

When asked to discuss our objections, I laid them out, explaining that building a reactor in China was tantamount to just handing them plans. I explained how Chinese firms have stolen or lifted American intellectual property for decades and that Westinghouse's proprietary nuclear technology would almost certainly be transferred to the People's Liberation Army to develop nuclear-powered equipment that would rival our ships and planes. I also stressed that one of the reasons America's submarines are so quiet and therefore harder to detect is that the nuclear technology we used was vastly superior to what the PLA currently had.

None of this seemed to matter. In fact, some of the representatives from the State Department and the US Nuclear Regulatory Commission, which are responsible for the 123 Agreements, looked at me like I was crazy.

In the end, the Joint Chiefs' recommendations were ignored. The powers that had been in the Obama administration overruled us. I have no idea who made the final decision or what their reasoning was. It is possible lobbyists applied pressure to influential members of Obama's cabinet. Or perhaps someone just thought that trade and revenue generation were more important than national security. If that was what happened, then it is another textbook case of America ignoring long-term potential damage in favor of short-term gains. That business-before-reality kind of thinking is our nation's own worst enemy and plays directly into our rivals' hands. But I saw it in action with even more dangerous results when I joined the National Security Council and began to plan for a game with much higher stakes.

CHAPTER FIVE

THE DIGITAL BATTLEFIELD

CHINA HAS REPLICATED ITS GEOGRAPHIC DEFENSIVE cocoon in cyberspace. Just as its remote distance from US allies protects it from military vulnerability, the great firewall of China serves as a digital fortress, a closed internet system that is difficult to attack. In the West, the internet was built for connectivity. China—in keeping with the CCP's rigid, authoritarian, thought-police mentality and driven by its understanding of data as a strategic weapon—constructed a cyber-defense system that can deny connectivity. In other words, its firewall exists to block and censor sites the CCP deems dangerous. Furthermore, if forces outside the firewall launch denial-of-service attacks, conduct targeted malware campaigns, or attempt any other hostile cyber assault—operations that the digital wing of the PLA performs every day—the Chinese authorities can deny access within China.

The People's Liberation Army is not a national army per se. It is the official security wing of the CCP. Therefore, PLA Unit 6139, the army's massive cyber warfare division, is a politically sanctioned hostile military force, built to blitz the West day in and day out. This cyber unit has become central to China's unrestricted warfare strategy. It is the weapon that allows China to say, "We are not going to use our armed forces at all. Instead, we'll use our cyber warriors as destabilizing agents to undermine rival economies and political systems." The goal? To obtain and use influence to force other nations to cede to its way of looking at the world—how to organize society, what rights citizens should have, what economic decisions that benefit China will be made.

To achieve this, China employs millions of its citizens as hackers and internet monitors. In 2008, numerous published reports revealed that the government was paying tens of thousands of citizens 50 Chinese cents (the equivalent of 7 US cents) each to write an individual post promoting party policy. The payment amount gave rise to a new phrase, the 50-Cent Party, which was used by critics to describe blind fealty to CCP policy.

By 2013, the numbers had swelled. Official Chinese media reported that the propaganda wing of the CCP had hired two million "public opinion analysts." That number has doubtless climbed, aided by an estimated ten million student volunteers who also engage in monitoring and disinformation work, both at home and on foreign websites. Meanwhile, the PLA's force of hackers launches assaults against US companies, government agencies, political parties.

Because of the diffuse nature of the internet, where a hacker in Beijing can route his computer to make it appear as if he is located in, say, Latvia, you might think it is difficult to ascertain where these attacks originate. But in many instances, the source is evident because of easily identifiable patterns to certain attacks. For example, American businesses have noticed that a cyber barrage will stop promptly at a set time every day: 11 P.M. in New York, which is lunchtime in China. An hour later, like clockwork, the Chinese cybernauts, having eaten, resume their attacks. And guess when the strikes stop for twelve- to fourteen-hour periods? At 4 A.M. eastern time—the end of the workday at the PLA's digital sabotage bunkers.

But the goals of the PLA are wide and varied. Stealing technical plans is great for specific purposes that—like building a sophisticated wind turbine or a patented chemical compound—can help destroy industry rivals, drive huge profits, and further strategic goals. But stealing data in bulk and accessing email can be even more valuable, unleashing a trove of information to be used broadly to achieve influence. At its most obvious level, accessing someone's emails or texts can be used for blackmail. We've seen this time and again in the West. Gaining access to nude photos and private messages that expose financial wrongdoing or embarrassing sexual shenanigans are obvious tools to increase influence. There are, however, many more subtle and complex operations going on.

When a hotel chain's customer database is compromised, when a company's employee directory is hacked, when credit reports are stolen, all these elements can be cross-indexed and mined to identify targets for influencing campaigns. Key corporate players can be identified. Their business trips can be tracked, exposing what companies might be working together or might be acquired—and any employees who are experiencing fiscal hardship. In this way, seemingly disparate data sets can provide actionable intelligence. Individuals and businesses can be targeted for strategic offensives to further CCP goals.

This may sound drastic and complex, but it is part and parcel of the theories espoused in *Unrestricted Warfare.* The bonding agent of data—what the book makes clear is the most potent weapon in the modern world—is an explosive substance. In the hands of the PLA, digital assaults to access data are both destructive—entrapping and disrupting the West by setting off digital landmines, raids, and intelligence operations—and constructive. The results of these operations—covertly harvested data—allow China to accrue influence and power. I have already detailed a complex, high-stakes cyber sabotage operation in the chapter examining economic warfare. Here are two smaller examples of China's surveillance and undue digital influence. What is particularly chilling is how unsuspecting and completely innocent Americans wound up caught in influencing power plays without even realizing it.

The Disturbing Case of Roy Jones

In January of 2018, a forty-nine-year-old man named Roy Jones was working at the customer-engagement center of Marriott International, in Omaha, Nebraska.

One day, while helping manage the company's Twitter feed, Jones saw that a Tibetan independence group had cited Marriott for listing Tibet as separate from China in a recent survey.

Using Marriott's official Rewards account, Jones liked the tweet.

That one click, which Jones later claimed he didn't remember making, set off a sad and infuriating chain of events. One in which a major American corporation crumbled in the face of pressure from China.

Although Twitter is banned in China, someone was clearly monitoring the feed maintained by the group promoting Tibetan independence and discovered two things: the Marriott chain had published a survey that might have implied Tibet was an independent country, and the Marriott Twitter feed "liked" the Tibet group's shout-out.

These "shocking" events were flagged to the Shanghai Municipal Tourism Administration, which contacted Marriott representatives to complain about the survey and the tweet. The tourism group then "ordered the company to publicly apologize and 'seriously deal with the people responsible,'" according to *The Wall Street Journal*.

Three days later, on January 14, 2018, Marriott fired Jones.

"I was completely unaware of what was going on," Jones told the *Journal*. "We were never trained in any of the social graces when it came to dealing with China."

And Marriott's corporate leadership, evidently, was never trained in defending its employees or standing up for free speech. Yes, the company has a fiduciary responsibility to stockholders. But it also has a responsibility to its employees and to the nation that has allowed Marriott to flourish.

Roy Jones wasn't just the victim of a poor management decision. He was the victim of China's social media surveillance capabilities and economic influence. What happened to him could, as we'll see, conceivably one day happen to any American anywhere who does something Chinese authorities don't like.

Football Fan Phishing

Thomas Everyman (not his real name) worked at a midsized tech company. Anyone looking at Everyman's LinkedIn page could learn his job title, the name of his employer, and the college he had attended. Anyone looking at his Facebook page could discover more personal details by looking at pages he had "liked." He was, for example, an avid booster of his alma mater's football team. Not only had Everyman liked the team's page; he had also identified himself as a follower of a fan newsletter devoted to the team.

This kind of personal information shouldn't seem particularly revealing or dangerous. But in the hands of hostile Chinese cyber forces, it was almost as good as having his sign-in name and password.

One day, Everyman got to work and noticed that a newsletter about the team had arrived in his email inbox. (His company email address, by the way, could be determined by a Google search for his employer's email format.) He opened it up. It looked just like the newsletter he subscribed to, and he started reading. An item contained a hyperlinked bit of text, linking to another article. But the item and the link were not what they seemed. They were part of a phishing attack. The item had been inserted by hackers. By clicking the item's accompanying link, Everyman unwittingly unleashed a malicious code that opened a path to the company's computer system and gave the Chinese hackers access to corporate plans, emails, technical specs. The company eventually realized that it had been compromised and hired an auditing firm to investigate. The firm traced the attack to Everyman's computer and pieced together how the employee had been targeted using publicly available information, a bit of cunning, and predatory technology.

In the end, China was able to gain all the company's product designs and customer lists, as well as research and development. It then used this information to build a new company that would soon outcompete Everyman's company, which is now struggling to survive.

As I said, these two stories involve average Americans just trying to live their lives who somehow got caught in China's relentless quest to steal and intimidate, to influence and dominate. Without extreme vigilance and pushback by the US government and US companies, there is nothing to stop this from happening to anybody.

Including you.

Redeployment

While the PLA has been organizing millions of Chinese to help on the digital battlefield, the US Army has been besieged with contractors, lobbyists, and politicians urging it to conduct business as usual. As Rep. Adam Smith, chairman of the House Armed Services Committee, told reporters; "I've got the idea that the military-industrial complex has the incentive to try to tell you that you need to spend more money on defense, but that incentive does not necessarily translate into national security needs; it simply translates into money."

Smith isn't wrong.

And what's worse is how the lobbying and vying for money is inefficient, misleading, and divisive. It takes our collective eye off the most pressing issues.

In August 2018, the US Cyber Command (CYBER-

COM), created in 2009, was made one of ten unified command units within the Pentagon. Its mission is defined as planning, coordinating, integrating, synchronizing, and conducting activities to "direct the operations and defense of specified Department of Defense information networks and; prepare to, and when directed, conduct full-spectrum military cyberspace operations in order to enable actions in all domains, ensure US/Allied freedom of action in cyberspace and deny the same to our adversaries."

That is a good start, but it is not enough. Given the modern-day realities and the size of the US economy, which runs through digital platforms, cyber protection needs to be paramount. CYBERCOM should become the sixth branch of the US Armed Forces, joining the Army, Air Force, Coast Guard, Marines, and Navy, with commensurate staffing and budget. It is that important.

We need battalions of digital warriors to protect our businesses and infrastructure. The defense of our nation's power grid is just as vital as the defense of our borders. Actually, it may be more so: without electricity, our society cannot function. Phones won't charge, computers will crash, life-support machines will fail, banks can't operate, cash registers won't ring, traffic lights won't work. People will perish.

The cyber-defense problem—like the problem of unchecked, irresponsible financing, like the problem of counterfeiting goods, like the problem of IP theft—has been kicked down the road by our leaders.

Meanwhile, the attacks of modern warfare—cyber war—continue daily.

What are we going to do about it?

Social Cyber Assault

Although the phrase "psychological warfare" is fairly recent, the concept has been around forever. A broad definition would be any verbal acts made to weaken an opponent by making them feel less confident, or instilling fear or division. The digital world has provided a massive, unsupervised platform for doing just that. The tools of predigital propaganda relied, in general, on two stages of deployment. First, ostensibly damaging information was put out into the world: pamphlets rained down, radio shows aired, articles ran, rumors were floated. Second, that information was shared and repeated. But other than bombarding a targeted population with messages, there was no way to gauge how effectively the propaganda was replicating. Fliers dropped from airplanes could be collected and burned without being read, or they could be passed hand to hand like sacred texts; there was no way of ensuring the outcome.

Now, in the unsupervised, unpoliced Wild West of the internet and social networks, psychological warfare has entered a new and potentially deadly realm. Social media is a tool to launch misinformation, division, and discord, to create false narratives, to destabilize, to interfere with the democratic process, to incite violence. It is a potent and subtle, almost undetectable form of poison. We've already seen what it can do to national events. Russia has been identified as the bad central actor in the 2016 US presidential election, taking active measures during the campaign to sway independent and undecided voters in swing states against Hillary Clinton.

While China has, as far as anyone knows, steered clear of meddling in the US elections, there is no question that it is committed to conducting influencing operations. This quote from a paper issued by the Cyberspace Administration of China's Theoretical Studies Center Group makes a case for ongoing assaults on behalf of the CCP:

> Enhance the guidance of online public opinion. Starting from the overall situation of the party and the state, effectively propagandize achievements in reform and development and economic livelihood and propaganda and provide policy interpretation on the economic situation. Alleviate doubts and boost confidence. *Actively use new technologies and new applications to effectively guide the progression of online public opinion, grasp the evolution and laws of the online public sentiment, prevent hot issues from involving the economic and social livelihood of the people, and prevent mass incidents and public opinion from becoming online ideological patterns and issues. Play an important role in cyber comments and public opinion guidance,*

> *and make cyberspace cleaner.* (Italics added for emphasis.)

This is a government policy agency stating that the country's cyber forces should engage in active propaganda to shape public opinion. The document, dizzyingly entitled "Deepening the Implementation of General Secretary Xi Jinping's Strategic Thinking on Building China into a Cyber Superpower: Steadily Advancing Cybersecurity and Informatization Work," is even more explicit about the end goal of web and social media posting: "Online positive publicity must become bigger and stronger, so that the Party's ideas always become the strongest voice in cyberspace."

Kathleen M. Carley is an academic pioneer in the science of social cyber security. Hired initially as a sociology professor at Carnegie Mellon University, she now works at the Institute for Software Research within CMU's School of Computer Science, where she studies, in a broad sense, the links between computation, organization, and society. More narrowly, she is now a leading academic in the study of social cyber warfare—how bad actors can use social networks like Twitter, Facebook, Reddit, Instagram, and other platforms to manipulate users, promote and influence political agendas, conduct disinformation campaigns, and sow division and conflict.

All social media platforms do two basic things, according to Carley and her researchers: provide users with access to particular individuals and access to particular content.

The platforms develop algorithmic prioritization schemes to determine what users see and what they read, as well as which messages are recommended and which other users are recommended as people to follow. Groups or nations that want to conduct influence campaigns construct messages and activate users—including programmed "bots"—to exploit the prioritization logic of these services. By creating an army of bots that like and repost messages to create an echo chamber of manipulative posts, bad actors can inject misinformation and sow division into a society with an unparalleled ferocity and speed.

It's a psychological warfare nightmare come true.

Carley confirmed China's intense interest in keeping social networks under surveillance, noting that a media lab at Beijing's Tsinghua University receives the entire feed of data from China's popular Weibo platform—that is, the posts, images, videos, memes, and metadata of its 450 million-plus users—to analyze.

This level of surveillance, Carley remarked, is one of the reasons people with surveillance concerns in China use virtual private networks (VPNs), which connect them to servers beyond what's known as the Great Firewall of China. VPNs allow users to send messages and make posts while avoiding the authorities' spying methods. It is also the reason that the CCP has banned Chinese websites from offering VPN apps and subscriptions.

Obtaining a social media platform's entire data set is a dream come true for anyone engaged in cyber social warfare. First, it allows you to map the entire social structure of the platform. You can see who is connected to whom. Second, by reverse engineering the data, you can ascertain the prioritization rules driving a platform: you can learn the criteria for ranking people on the platform, and how their posts and likes and comments are weighted; how reposting gains traction, how tagging can help expand the reach of a post. This information can then inform and optimize future cyber warfare operations for maximum impact. Or, as Carley puts it, "They basically construct messages and fake groups so they can exploit the prioritization logic of these technologies."

Having access to the content before the algorithms are applied to it is also something that concerns Carley: "If it flows to you before it arrives where it was supposed to be going, you could actually put in deep fakes. You could alter the routing and affect the dissemination."

You could edit the content of someone's post, too.

Expanding Global Influence

While much of Carley's work has centered on tracking Russian campaigns to sow division and inflame tensions in the United States and Britain, in 2019 she began to examine how social media was being manipulated to influence national elections in the Philippines and Indonesia—two countries that are relatively close to China.

In the Philippines, a nation that until recently had historically strong ties to the United States (and that has the fourth-largest population of English speakers in the world), President Rodrigo Duterte wrangled a pledge of $24 billion in investment, credit, and loans from China to upgrade his country's infrastructure. Since the agreement was announced in 2016, few upgrades have happened, and Duterte has come under fire for both overpromising and underdelivering, and for being duped by China.

"What we're seeing is an increase in the use of bots in the [2016] election, supporting Rodrigo Duterte and supporting the infrastructure development and these contracts," Carley says. "I can't actually trace the IP address and say, 'Definitely, I can guarantee that's coming from China.' But those are certainly activities in the Chinese interest."

Similarly, social media research in Indonesia, where Twitter is hugely popular, has detected bot activity pushing the candidacy of incumbent president Joko "Jokowi" Widodo and his cronies, Carley reports. As head of the world's most populous Muslim nation, Widodo has been conspicuously silent about China's persecution of its Muslim Uighur population. But he has not been shy about meeting five times with President Xi or welcoming Chinese investment, which increased 300 percent from 2015 to 2016, according to *This Week in Asia*. His government, as a 2018 AP report put it, "is reluctant to publicly criticize Beijing, fearing it could jeopardize potential Chinese investment."

If China is conducting influencing operations in Indonesia, it appears to be much more subtle than the Russian efforts. "It definitely seems like they're not trying to sell division too hard," says Carley. "They're definitely trying to shore up [a message] that 'we're the good guys. You should like us. You should like our approach, our approach works better.'"

That strategy hews close to techniques we'll discuss in an upcoming chapter about politics and diplomacy: the Chinese are very good at twisting the narrative to make you think they are genuinely acting in your own best interests, and at convincing everybody to trust them.

Of course, when it comes to trust issues, there may be no bigger game on the planet than 5G.

CHAPTER SIX

MODERN WARFARE 5.0: THE 5G FUTURE

IN 2014, DEPUTY SECRETARY OF DEFENSE ROBERT Work was put in charge of the Defense Innovation Initiative. This project was heralded as the "Third Offset strategy," a phrase that drew on two of the most successful plans in US military history. The First Offset was Eisenhower's use of nuclear deterrence to counteract the Soviet Union's lead in conventional arms. The Second Offset—started by Defense Secretary Harold Brown and Undersecretary of Defense for Research and Engineering William Perry in the Carter administration and continued by Reagan—called for investment in superior technologies, such as stealth aircraft, precision-guided missiles, and satellite spying. It is worth mentioning that these weapons were built using research and design breakthroughs of the 1960s and 1970s that were funded by the Pentagon. Back then, about 2 percent of America's GDP was spent on R&D. Today, we spend about 0.7 percent. Taken together, the first two offsets contributed to the fall of the Soviet empire.

The Third Offset—"an ambitious department-wide effort to identify and invest in innovative ways to sustain and advance America's military dominance for the 21st century," according to Obama administration secretary of defense Chuck Hagel—was going to leverage American technical innovation. It was necessary, Hagel added, because "while we spent over a decade focused on grinding stability operations, countries like Russia and China have been heavily investing in military modernization programs to blunt our military's technological edge."

When Robert Work started trying to implement the Defense Innovation Initiative, he and Hagel's replacement, Ash Carter, were in for a rude awakening. The Pentagon assumed that it would work with tech companies and share resources to build new cutting-edge weapons systems. But China had already thoroughly infiltrated the tech space with investments and scientists. We failed to realize that the Chinese were involved in all those commercial research partnerships. There were pacts with Google and partnerships with Apple. Chinese scientists often worked side by side with our scientists—even on research and development for the US military. With these arrangements, any work performed on behalf of the US military was likely going to be done by or shared with Chinese scientists.

In other words, the introduction of the internet inexorably linked economic security with our national security. We could no longer think about Silicon Valley's growth model as independent of our national security. In raising the alarm from inside government, I learned firsthand how firmly China's strategy was enabled by our own fixed notions of the separation of business and government, the separation of economic and national security. I also learned personally how hard the industry lobby would fight to defend its ability to maintain this dangerous status quo. More on that later.

As for the start-up market, where cutting-edge applications and innovation flourish, China remained focused on locking up early-stage tech deals, too. In 2015, Chinese investors participated "in 271 deals, with total deal value of $11.5 billion," according to a report issued by the Defense Innovation Unit Experimental, which noted, "This represented almost 16% of the value of all technology deals in that year ($72 billion)."

The Air Force's state-of-the-art stealth bomber, the F-35, a highly computerized machine built with systems accessible from the ground, is a victim of China's infiltration of US technology. Some of the parts used to build F-35s are actually manufactured in China. In this instance, the supply chain becomes a huge vulnerability, and not just the secrets the manufacturers are given access to are at risk—the plane itself is. Army intelligence has concluded that the Chinese stole all the plans for the F-35. Now you have to wonder about sabotaged parts that might destroy the machine or, worse, the idea that components contain backdoor access to the plane's operating system. In this scenario, it is conceivable that the plane could be taken down or hacked. We might lose command and control of our own asset.

So the United States has the most versatile and agile stealth flying machine in the world, and we can't trust it, because we don't have the secure digital pipes we need to ensure that the correct data flows in safely, dependably, without exposure to hacking.

Which brings me to the matter of 5G, the groundbreaking fifth-generation modern communications paradigm.

The 5G platform is not like 2G or 3G or even 4G. Not even close. It is not just a mobile phone network built to connect phone calls, email, and text messages.

Think of it as the next generation of the internet, built for machines.

It is, not to put too fine a point on it, one hundred times faster than 4G. That means there will be almost no latency—no delay—between sending and receiving data on 5G.

So 5G is a much faster, more direct, more precise platform that allows nearly instantaneous communication between people, between machines, and between people and machines. That speed and precision mean 5G will transform our society in ways that are hard to fathom. It is a strategist's job, however, to look toward the future and explore possible outcomes. It is clear that technological advances will accelerate well beyond the current pace, as data will be able to flow from apps and sensors, feeding machine learning and artificial intelligence engines. Accentuating the positive, it is easy to imagine 5G improving many facets of modern life. Surgeries might be able to be performed remotely by doctors or even by machines. And machines—cars in need of brake pads, home furnaces in need of cleaning, air conditioners in need of filters, lamps in need of lightbulbs—will be able to self-regulate and notify owners or managers when they need servicing. Furthermore, dangerous jobs, such as unsafe mining operations, deep-sea salvage, or the sterilization of clinics during an Ebola outbreak—may be done using remote robots.

But for all the promise of this new, completely wireless world—and yes, even the once-vital transcontinental fiber optic lines lying on the ocean floor may be rendered obsolete by the power of 5G—the new network will bring new vulnerabilities, new security worries, and new national concerns. Defending against these security threats should fall, at least in part, to the military. But ironically, the military needs to be defended, too; if the communications system used by our national defenses is penetrated, our nation's safety will be compromised.

When I joined the National Security Council in May 2017, I had two goals in mind: educate the other members of the NSC on China's not-so-covert campaign for global dominance, and ensure the security of the 5G network not only within US borders but for our allies as well. Given decades of Chinese digital infiltration and IP theft, there was little doubt that the CCP would put a premium on controlling 5G networks. China's biggest telecom companies, Huawei and ZTE, began aggressively offering to build 5G networks for other nations. And that set off alarm bells in my head.

If a Chinese telecom builds and controls a nation's 5G network, there will be no checks and balances to keep the Chinese company from stealing and mining all the data on that network: all the academic papers and research, all engineering and business plans, all the photos, emails, and text messages. Everything will be fair game to a country that doesn't believe in fair games. Furthermore, controlling another nation's network will allow the CCP to weaponize the technology that is managed by the network. What does that mean? Think of a hostile force taking over a self-driving car or bus and directing it to crash into a crowded sidewalk. Think of a flock of drones moving into the flight path of an airplane. Think of every digitally controlled furnace shutting down during a subzero cold spell.

The blend of technologies and spectrums behind 5G will allow for about three million connected devices per square mile. This is an exponential upgrade from 4G, which enables about ten thousand connections per square mile. That means that in a stadium hosting an NFL football game, every smartphone-owning fan in attendance will have a network connection, but so will any drones, sensors, or robots in or near the stadium—including the cars in the parking lot. The capacity for communication offered by 5G is stunning. It is much better to think of 5G as a network built for machines, since most of the network traffic will eventually be machine to machine. This will allow for massive data production, which will feed machine learning and artificial intelligence algorithms, which in turn will continue improving the technology in a giant information feedback loop.

The societal implications of 5G—on how we live and how we work—are truly mind-boggling.

And so is the capacity to abuse that power.

Let's be totally clear: *Anything connected to an unsecured 5G network will be a potential weapon that can be used to gain geopolitical influence and control. If China were to control a 5G network, it would be able to weaponize the technology within entire cities—or entire countries—served by that network and hold that city or state at its mercy.*

The NSC is run by the national security adviser, who has an office in the West Wing of the White House. Most of his staff, the council, operates out of the old Executive Office, now known as the Eisenhower Executive Office Building, just west of the White House. The council, as you'd imagine, is filled with experts. Some are Middle East experts. Some are Russia experts. Some are Europe experts. Some are nuclear weapons experts. Naturally, every expert thinks his area of focus is of paramount importance, myself included. But if the NSC is concerned with clear and present danger—which is part of its mandate—I knew to my core that the biggest threat to national security wasn't ISIS, Al Qaeda, and radical Islam or Vladimir Putin. It was and is China. And nothing would be more damaging than the CCP's potential global dominance of 5G networks. I intended to make this clear to the entire NSC.

Unfortunately, because of internal politics, I didn't have the clout to push my understanding of China's strategy to the forefront of the NSC. So I crafted a way to build awareness of China's threat to security indirectly. I organized a series of open forums I called "Winning without War" and invited the entire NSC to attend. I booked speakers to discuss economic warfare, political warfare, information warfare, and legal warfare—different ways that you can defeat an opponent without actually firing a shot. The forums each consisted of a forty-five-minute presentation, a twenty-minute Q and A, and then a forty-five-minute free-for-all discussion.

For the first meeting, I asked James Mulvenon, a longtime China hand and coauthor of 2013's *Chinese Industrial Espionage*, to talk. The effect was electric: total engagement. Many of the Trump administration who were interested in China policy were there. By the end of the meeting, things got really heated. At one point, a China watcher basically called a military policy expert a panda-hugger, and all hell broke loose. This was not business as usual at the NSC.

To keep the peace, I got up and gave the last word. I thanked everyone for attending and said I had two observations: "The first thing that we need to do is realize that the enemy is not in this room; it's six thousand miles away. And the second thing is that the truth is, we've all been alcoholics, essentially getting drunk on China. What are we going to do about it?"

The talks were well attended and extremely influential. I believe they led to an invitation to contribute to the 2018 National Security Strategy and help lay out our China policy and our 5G policy.

I began drafting a memo about the future of 5G in the United States. In it, I stated that the creation of the network was a national security issue—as opposed to a business or technology issue. The paper asserted that protecting the security of our 5G network was critical to stopping Chinese influence and hostile actions. And because that was critical to maintaining our levels of security and freedom, the effort should be led by the US government.

The document outlined a plan to transition to a wholesale model for wireless communications. The idea was that the United States would share the military spectrum with a private company that would construct and maintain a secure 5G network and then lease out bandwidth to retail providers. By providing a secure option in which communications would be encrypted and protected, and allowing telecoms to procure and provide access to the network, we would ensure the integrity of our information and communications infrastructure and begin to break China's telecommunications-market dominance.

In my proposal, I compared a government build-out of

5G to Eisenhower's national highway plan, a giant infrastructure plan that sought to ensure the swift movement of military troops, hardware, and ancillary support through the country. Yes, it opened up the nation and jump-started the long-distance trucking industry, but the multibillion-dollar highway project was rooted in infrastructure and security. The 5G platform is no different. It is about building a highway, too—an information highway.

Although my analogy was rooted in history, the proposal was greeted as a radical idea in many quarters. Telecommunications in America has been owned and operated by the private sector for more than one hundred years. The multibillion-dollar industry regarded the idea of government involvement—other than the breakup of AT&T's monopoly in the 1970s—as antithetical to free trade and therefore inconceivable.

The idea that the government would be overstepping its bounds, however, flies in the face of precedent and reality. The government of the United States controls or regulates many markets of national importance. Airlines are subject to the rules and requirements of the Federal Aviation Administration, which oversees the skies of America. The Nuclear Regulatory Commission licenses and inspects reactors. The Food and Drug Administration dictates which drugs can and can't be sold. The federal government even controls the price of milk! Airlines, nuclear power, drugs, and food—those are four vital industries with government regulation that I was able to name off the top of my head. I'm sure there are plenty of others. So the argument that the government would be overregulating by managing or "overseeing" 5G to ensure national security and safety is entirely disingenuous. That's precisely what a government should do. And I say that as someone with libertarian leanings.

My proposal was leaked to the press. I have no idea who was behind the disclosure, but it set off a firestorm of criticism. Sources have told me that representatives of a large American telecom put pressure on the administration to get rid of me.

Apparently, those sources were correct. That same week, I received word that my "detail was ended." That was the system's way of saying I was being removed—in effect, fired—from my position at the NSC.

My bid to awaken the NSC and to ensure that America can operate safely and securely in the future was over. On one level, I was okay with leaving the NSC. I had succeeded in getting a 5G declaration placed in the 2018 National Security Strategy document signed by President Trump: "We will improve America's digital infrastructure by deploying a secure 5G Internet capability nationwide."

I also felt that I had succeeded in awakening the NSC to China's stealth war. My goal was to get people to understand the problem, because that is the first step toward formulating good policy.

But on another level, nobody likes being forced out of a job. That was frustrating. The scariest, most disheartening thing of all, however, was the thought—the reality, actually—that after more than twenty years serving my country, I was bounced, in part, so that corporations could sacrifice long-term national security for quick and easy short-term profits.

This has become the American way.

It has to change.

Now.

CHAPTER SEVEN

POLITICS AND DIPLOMACY

"WAR IS A MERE CONTINUATION OF POLICY BY other means."

Carl von Clausewitz, a German military theorist, wrote those words two centuries ago. He was referring to "public policy," another name for "politics." Military scholars, then, generally interpret this statement as saying that "politics" and "war" are synonymous. And that means politics can be viewed as a continuation of war by other means.

This makes perfect sense where China is concerned. What Clausewitz is saying—that war is a political act or a political decision used to drive an outcome in the winner's favor—can be applied to the CCP's strategy. The CCP uses political and diplomatic engagement and deception to gain control and expand China's spheres of influence without going to war. This echoes the brilliant central idea of both Sun Tzu's *The Art of War* and *Unrestricted Warfare*: to get what you want without going into battle. The Chinese have absorbed this lesson. They understand the risks and damage of war. For thousands of years, they have been farmers, not fighters. They built the Great Wall to try to eliminate war. So their solution is to pick up on Clausewitz's theory and sort of turn it on its head. China says, "War? We are not going to play that game." Instead, China views politics and diplomacy as the battlefield, although it takes pains not to seem like the aggressor. The CCP uses guile, cunning, bribery, and bargaining to achieve desired outcomes. Or, to put it in real-world terms, its entire strategy is built around political influence, information, and buying people off.

The heart of political and diplomatic warfare—influencing—is a two-step process. First, it requires knowing who pulls the levers—that is, who has the clout to make things happen. Second, it requires getting those people to do your dirty work by convincing them that they are serving their own best interests. In other words, Chinese diplomacy seeks to manipulate targets so they don't realize they are doing the CCP's dirty work. To do this, China convinces other countries that it is a good neighbor or partner and is genuinely trying to help their partners help themselves. There is little doubt that this ploy drives the vast majority of deals as China unfurls its projected $1.3 trillion Belt and Road infrastructure plan for developing nations. By building a global network of connected railroads, highways, and ports throughout two-thirds of the world, China can talk a great game about helping countries participate in the worldwide economy. But it also puts the CCP in a position to control that economy and exploit all the data that is generated as people and goods move around the world.

"No conflict. No confrontation. Win-win cooperation" is the CCP's sly slogan.

The same "trust us and let us help you" idea is used again and again as China strikes deals all over the globe, and as it offers to build deep ports, as it has in Sri Lanka, Pakistan, Greece, and other nations. It's easy to see how a developing nation can be lured by what might seem like favorable terms and generous revenue projections, all pitched at strengthening its economy. It's easy to imagine that nation's leaders saying, "This is good for our . . . ," while Chinese diplomats nod in agreement. What is rarely discussed is how the leaders entering these agreements may also benefit from kickbacks, sweetheart side deals, and other enticements. If you can convince someone that the things that they're doing are in their own best interest, then that's the easiest way to get them to act.

Just ask any con man. He'll tell you the same thing.

If you can align your rival's motives politely, without any coercion, by subtle influence and clever words, by offering access to money, or by wielding false information that masks onerous terms, you are winning the war.

The word "diplomacy" has evolved. Today, it conjures up images of careful, polite negotiation, but it hasn't always been viewed that way. Diplomacy is conducted, of course, by diplomats, and that brings up another worthy, centuries-old quote: "An ambassador is an honest man sent to lie abroad for the good of his country." This line was uttered by a man who personified the dignified image of diplomacy: Sir Henry Wotton was a poet and art connoisseur who served as England's ambassador to Venice in the early seventeenth century.

China uses both forms of diplomacy. Ideally, it relishes operating behind the scenes when it comes to negotiation. While transparency is a hallmark of good governance in the West, discussing policy in public—issuing statements to the media—is something Chinese diplomats actively discourage. When I began working as a military attaché in Beijing, I was told by the Chinese that making policy issues public was tantamount to "offending the feelings of 1.4 billion Chinese people." That, of course, is absurd. How is publicly discussing any international issue an offense? And yet, when I arrived at the Joint Chiefs of Staff, this attitude of not publicly calling China out on issues had permeated the US federal government. I don't know if this policy was in place during the Clinton or Bush administrations—although I suspect that it was, given their inaction on China—but the instructions from the Obama administration were loud and clear: we are not going to do anything in public to antagonize China, as the relationship is too significant financially. The narrative was that the two most powerful countries in the world had to cooperate and get along to solve great challenges, like North Korea and climate change.

That stance was built on the absurd idea that China wants to fix either of these issues. It doesn't.

North Korea's leader, Kim Jong-un, lives and breathes by the will of the CCP, which loves having him act like a totalitarian madman and divert attention away from the Beijing government's oppressive actions. This is no exaggeration. An estimated fifty thousand North Koreans are working daily in Chinese factories, basically funding an underground economy in North Korea. And when it comes to Kim building intercontinental ballistic missiles, who, logically, would have supplied his broke and embargoed nation with those plans?

As for the environment and climate change, China's overfishing is destroying fisheries across the globe. When its trawlers are caught red-handed in foreign waters, it issues denials or announces increased vigilance, but the next day, Chinese ships are out raiding the ocean again. Meanwhile, China remains the world's worst polluter, spewing more carbon into the air than any other nation on earth. But even in this realm, it sidesteps the rules. One brilliant thing China has done, tactically speaking, is build coal-fired electricity plants in neighboring countries, including Russia, then pipe the energy across the border. So China can claim it is reducing the amount of carbon it generates—by outsourcing the problem across the border—while it remains responsible for poisoning the air as much, if not more, than ever.

The carbon maneuver underscores how China has mastered the other form of diplomacy: spin. Chinese diplomats focus on good optics, portraying their positions as helpful, issuing sound bites that ooze with goodwill, and hosting elaborate conferences and junkets designed to showcase their generosity and do-good visions. But these carefully constructed exchanges are often distractions, misdirections, or total lies designed to disarm suspicion and sway popular opinion. While the Russians practice atomization, breaking down societies into rival groups, the Chinese practice obfuscation, clouding and cloaking behaviors. It's the opposite of transparency. Policy moves are conducted in secret, motives hidden, until deals are signed, sealed, and delivered. These two philosophies of influence—one loud, one quiet—actually work in tandem: Russia's activity serves as a distraction while China waltzes out the back door with the loot.

Finally, in the event that diplomacy fails and the friendly overtures of contract offers, trade terms, payouts, and infrastructure-building deals fall through, the old methods, such as intimidation, bullying, bribery, misinformation, and extortion, can get the job done.

Such tactics have more to do with thuggery than diplomacy. But the ends—increasing the CCP's influence over not just foreign governments and corporations but also media outlets, religious groups, academics, civil rights groups, and, at a frighteningly granular level, individual citizens—justify the means. Sadly, none of these bullying practices should surprise anyone. These diplomats and influence peddlers represent a country that routinely ignores international trade laws, property laws, environmental laws, drug laws, and pretty much any other law that stands in its way.

"The first rule of unrestricted warfare," said Col. Qiao Liang, coauthor of the book on the subject, explaining the strategy he envisioned, "is that there are no rules, with nothing forbidden."

Welcome to Chinese diplomacy.

Influencing Influencers

China pushes two levers to quietly achieve diplomatic influence: access to Chinese markets and access to money. In the United States, the lure of access to Chinese markets has been cast year after year. As we've discussed, it's been pretty clear that China has used this as a carrot on a stick to drive Wall Street and the investment community into a fever dream of future earnings. These visions are fantasies as long as China insists that earnings must remain in China. When China does disperse huge sums of money in America, it is to gain information, technology, or influence.

To wield those two weapons effectively, China's diplomatic wing has distilled its mission into two tasks: identifying people of influence and then swaying them. Tellingly, these guidelines are not that different from the rules driving many intelligence and counterintelligence operations to develop spies. For the CCP, ideal targets are people with political clout who either make decisions or advise people who make decisions. At the highest levels, CCP diplomats woo the presidents, prime ministers, and cabinet leaders of foreign governments. In the United States, Chinese operatives—businessmen, journalists, students, and military officers, as well as members of the Chinese embassy in Washington, DC, or its mission in New York—zoom in on senators, members of Congress, and military officers for influence operations. But to reach those targets, they may also reach out to a senator's wife. Or the employer of a senator's wife. Or, as in the case of Joe Biden, a vice president's son.

Engagement is a crucial requirement for influencing operations. It may start with a meeting invitation, an offer to share a meal or attend a conference, or an offer to launch a joint venture. From there, relationships build and deals are struck. Sometimes, these influencing operations can be blatantly obvious, such as the deal to back Hunter Biden's investment fund with $1 billion.

There are plenty of targets for China influencers. For instance, there are 100 senators and 435 members of the House of Representatives, and every single one of them, for various reasons, is interested in money and access to foreign markets.

A DC Dancer

On November 8, 2017, Montana senator Steve Daines issued a press release proudly announcing that he had secured a deal between the Montana Stockgrowers Association and

JD.com, one of China's largest retailers, which had agreed to purchase a minimum of $200 million in Montana-sourced beef over the next several years. The deal marked an end to China's ban on buying meat from American ranchers, which had been in effect since 2003. The agreement also included another boon for Montana's cattle industry: JD.com pledged "to seek to invest up to another $100 million" to build a processing plant in Big Sky Country. Never mind that the wording of that phrase means JD.com isn't obligated to spend a dime on a processing plant (and hadn't, according to a July 2018 *China Daily* report). If you didn't think about it too much, it sure sounded good.

At the end of the press release, Daines listed eighteen meetings and actions he had taken to make this happen, including trips to China, meetings with the Chinese ambassador, and meetings with Secretary of State Rex Tillerson, US Trade Representative Robert Lighthizer, and Commerce Secretary Wilbur Ross. In other words, he was doing his job and trying to serve the people of Montana, right?

It's more complicated than that.

Less than one month later, Daines hosted a delegation of CCP legislators who oversaw "the People's Congress of China's Tibet Autonomous Region." The visit, complete with beaming photo opportunity, was clearly timed to offset something else going on in town—specifically, a DC visit by Tibetan leader Lobsang Sangay, who was meeting with lawmakers and attending a December 6 House Foreign Affairs Asia subcommittee hearing on Chinese repression in Tibet.

Sangay, viewed as an enemy by the CCP, was on hand to put pressure on China to give foreign diplomats the same access to Tibet that Chinese officials who oversee Tibet enjoy on visits to the United States.

As a *Washington Post* columnist reported, "The episode illustrated China's growing practice of enlisting Western politicians to blunt criticism of the regime—and also its determination to haunt its opponents wherever they travel. 'Everywhere I go, I'm followed by a high-level Chinese delegation denying human rights abuses in Tibet,' Sangay told [the paper], adding that Chinese officials pressure governments across the world not to meet . . . with him."

There is nothing beyond circumstantial evidence to suggest that Daines's meeting was the result of a formal quid pro quo agreement with China. But the cause and effect seem apparent. After receiving $200 million in business for his state, he helped China blunt negative press over its repressive, undemocratic, and unrelenting control over Tibet.

Silencing the Voice of America

Sometimes China has been able to apply pressure to silence dissent—even right here in free-speech-loving America. And just when it looks like nothing more than political pressure, the dark shadow of money clouds events. Sasha Gong, a journalist who was the chief of Mandarin service for the Voice of America (VOA), learned this the hard way in 2017 when she scheduled an interview with Chinese billionaire Guo Wengui, who also goes by the name Miles Kwok.

Guo is a controversial figure, both at home and abroad. He made his money developing real estate. In 2014, he fled China and became a vocal critic of CCP leadership, accusing top leaders of rampant corruption and self-dealing. He named names and launched blockbuster charges; some have been substantiated, others have not. He also became a critic of the CCP's human rights abuses. The combination of his wealth, insider knowledge, and shocking tales of abuse made him one of the most intriguing figures operating outside China's borders. So he was a natural subject for Gong to approach.

Guo was interested in talking to the Voice of America. The government-funded news service is rarely heard within US borders. But since launching in 1942, it has engaged an enormous worldwide audience and has added digital and TV programming to its 24/7 lineup of radio broadcasts. Its operations are guided by a three-point charter that President Ford signed into law in 1976:

1. VOA will serve as a consistently reliable and authoritative source of news. VOA news will be accurate, objective, and comprehensive.
2. VOA will represent America, not any single segment of American society, and will therefore present a balanced and comprehensive projection of significant American thought and institutions.

3. VOA will present the policies of the United States clearly and effectively, and will also present responsible discussions and opinion on these policies.

Despite that nothing-but-truth-and-balance mission, Guo was concerned about how he would be portrayed in the interview. He had been unhappy with the way a recent BBC piece about him had been edited, and he told Gong he would agree to an interview if it was broadcast live. Gong responded with her own request for a three-hour interview, with the first hour beaming live on the radio and the next two hours broadcast via the internet. She also insisted on having a day of interviews with Guo on background so she and a coanchor could ensure that the presentation would be well structured and balanced. Guo agreed. When Gong told her boss at the VOA, she was congratulated for pulling off a coup.

The scheduled project was a one-hour simulcast on satellite TV and VOA internet channels, followed by a two-hour web-only engagement during which Guo would respond to questions posted on social media. It required the involvement of about sixty people at the VOA, according to Gong, including the publicity team, a social media specialist, producers, sound engineers, camera operators, lighting techs, and travel and logistics personnel. The project must have been signed off on, Gong notes, because "I sure did not have the power to arrange all this."

The interview was scheduled to take place live at Guo's

luxurious apartment on the top floor of the Sherry-Netherland hotel on New York's Fifth Avenue. It would begin at 9 A.M. ET on April 19, 2017. Given the twelve-hour time difference, it would air in China during prime time, at 9 P.M. On Friday, April 14, the VOA released a promotional spot. It publicized the exclusive interview and touted that Guo had promised "to deliver nuclear-level exposé," according to Gong.

It's important to note that the CCP controls the media in China. It also owns most Chinese-language foreign media outlets around the globe. So dissidents like Guo are literally almost never given airtime either within China or on government-owned channels that target the Chinese diaspora, such as the China Global Television Network, which broadcasts on cable networks here in the United States. So the VOA, by interviewing Guo, was providing him with a rare large platform to reach the Chinese-speaking world—a platform the CCP consistently denies to pro-democracy dissidents.

No one that Gong worked with at the VOA voiced any concern to her about dramatically hyping the interview. Evidently, they were aware of the journalistic value of the Guo scoop and that promoting a story is what media outlets do when they have a big exclusive.

But the promo was clearly monitored by authorities in China. The following Monday—the first business day after the promo aired—Chinese authorities announced an arrest warrant for Guo. He had fled China in 2014. But now that he was scheduled to beam into Chinese airwaves and possibly criticize the CCP, the government was formally moving to silence him.

Meanwhile, two members of the Chinese foreign ministry paid a visit to the VOA correspondent in Beijing. He sent an email to Gong, reporting that his visitors had said the CCP believed that by airing the Guo interview, the VOA was interfering with internal affairs and with the 19th Communist Party Congress. "When I read this," Gong recalls, "I said, 'How the hell is interviewing a businessman interfering with the Party Congress?' I called the office and I said, 'Tell them to go to hell. I don't care about this threat.'"

A senior editor voiced concerns about making sure the interview was balanced—a well-meaning but demeaning suggestion to Gong, who has been a journalist for years. "I said, 'Don't worry about it. I know how to be balanced.'"

The VOA offices were then hit with an onslaught of phone calls from the Chinese embassy in DC. "One editor called me and asked what to do. I said, 'What are they saying?' The editor told me they said, 'If you do the interview, it will permanently damage the relationship between the Chinese government and the Voice of America.'"

"I said just tell them Voice of America has no relationship with the Chinese government except we cover you. We report on you."

The final twenty-four hours before the interview was set to air were a nightmare for Gong. She recounts an epic screaming match with VOA deputy director Sandy Sugawara, who asked her to cancel the interview. An intimidating crowd of Chinese men followed Gong when she left Guo's apartment. Later, the program's executive producer told her she'd refused a request to air a fifteen-minute live interview and prepare a thirty-minute tape. During all this, Gong, who suffers from high blood pressure, worried she might need to be hospitalized. Finally, the day ended with a conference call with seven VOA editors and administrators in two languages, in which no one agreed to take responsibility for pulling the interview. "All these people were so cowardly," Gong recalls. "They could not even give one word to make the order. They wanted *me* to make the order. I'm not going to do that."

As all this behind-the-scenes drama was unfolding, the director of the VOA, Amanda Bennett, was touring Africa. Had the calls from the Chinese embassy made it through to her office? It seems likely, given all the other VOA offices that had been called. Furthermore, insiders note, Bennett, a seasoned journalist, had tangential connections to Beijing. Her husband, Donald Graham, the former publisher of the *Washington Post*, is the chairman of Graham Holdings Company, the owner of education services company Kaplan Inc., which has a division in China. Given that China sends more foreign students to the United States than any other country in the world, it is presumably a huge market opportunity for Kaplan.

Sometime after midnight, just hours before the scheduled interview, reports from inside China claimed that Beijing had issued a "code red" warrant for Guo's immediate arrest by Interpol. Gong now wondered whether her subject would be available and whether they'd even be able to access the equipment they'd placed in Guo's apartment.

They arrived to discover that the reports were bogus. Guo had heard nothing, and Interpol hadn't received a request. Two minutes before the interview was to start, the entire internet connection for the Sherry-Netherland, the luxurious building where Guo lived, crashed. According to Gong, the FBI later determined that a hacker in Shanghai had attacked the building. Fortunately, the VOA team had its own battery-powered transmitters, and the broadcast went on as scheduled.

Gong's broadcast went on for one hour and fifteen minutes. And then was shut down. According to Gong, the decision was made by Bennett. Gong and other members of the Guo broadcast team were suspended soon after the broadcast. Months later, Gong and two of her team were officially fired.

A letter from the VOA to Gong dated November 29, 2018, asserted that her "actions were intentional, unforgettable [sic] and harmful to the well-being of the Agency" and accused her of ignoring instructions "given by the uppermost and most senior employees of the agency."

That same day, Bennett released an email to the VOA staffers stating that the dismissals followed "four independent investigations that all concluded the interview's termination was a result of VOA leadership's attempt to enforce previously agreed-upon journalistic standards. The investigations found no evidence to support allegations that pressure from the Chinese government, purportedly driven by 'spies' within VOA, had caused the termination."

The email further stated:

> VOA leadership issued specific instructions to the interview team to (1) limit the interview to no more than one hour, (2) prohibit any extension of the interview over social media, (3) prohibit any use of unverified documentation or materials during the broadcast, (4) continue to tape the interview for as long as necessary to produce material for later, properly vetted, broadcast.

Gong says she has no illusions about what happened. She believes that the Voice of America was silenced and intimidated by Chinese government pressure: "I am quite convinced that Bennett was subjected to Chinese influence, because it made no sense, professionally speaking, for her to intervene in my interview so decisively and strongly, especially because she and her deputy had no idea about the content of the interview."

As for the pressure applied to Bennett, Gong alluded to Bennett's husband's business interests in China: "The Chinese created a new way of legal bribery. They don't need to pay for agents, just give them business opportunities."

Regardless of the countercharges of insubordination and influencing, the story itself is shocking. The premier American government news organization censored its coverage because, apparently, broadcasting an interview that contained criticism of the Chinese government was somehow not up to journalistic standards. Giving voice to the opposition is something that the VOA has done for decades. But in the wake of complaints from our greatest rival—and biggest trading partner—the opposition was silenced.

Influence Infiltration

Although China has been targeting developing nations all over the world—from the Congo to El Salvador, from the Philippines to Greece—with diplomatic initiatives that result in direct cash infusions, infrastructure investment, and other goodies, it has not been ignoring the United States. Not by a long shot.

Since 2004, the Chinese government has been funding Confucius Institutes (CIs) at American universities. The vast majority of these centers provide Mandarin language instruction for these schools and are staffed with teachers from China. While the institutes also frequently offer cultural programming and other services, including outreach classes for K–12 students in local schools, the big win for most colleges is a robust language program that administrators can effectively outsource with minimal expense. Officially, China insists that the CIs are nonprofit public institutions devoted to promoting Chinese language and culture in foreign countries. And that party line has been effective. The lure of low-cost quality language instruction has been a strong selling point. There were more than ninety CIs in place at American colleges and universities by 2017 and more than five hundred around the globe.

But the party line is a bunch of b.s. While every center is administered by codirectors, one appointed by China and one by the school, frequent reports of censorship and a lack of academic freedom emanate from CIs.

No such report was more disturbing, perhaps, than a decision by North Carolina State University to cancel a scheduled visit by the Dalai Lama, Tibet's exiled religious and political leader, after the school's Confucius Institute director warned the event might harm "strong relationships we were developing with China."

Was that a concern or a threat? Judging by the cancellation, the administration evidently took it as a threat that would hurt the university, and it caved to pressure.

There have been other reports of censorious behavior and manipulation stemming from CIs. The Chinese CI co-director at the University of Albany in New York pulled down posters about Taiwan before his bosses from the Chinese Ministry of Education showed up. A US Senate subcommittee report noted that in one state with a number of K-12 Confucius classrooms, an email was sent warning against booking a drama company with ties to Falun Gong, the spiritual group banned in China. "For those schools who've recently been awarded Confucius Classroom funds, please note that they may not be used to support attendance at, or sponsoring of, Shen Yun performances."

Ten years after the first Confucius Institute, at the University of Maryland, opened its doors, the American Association of University Professors issued a report denouncing the centers for engaging in academic censorship. The report urged universities to shutter the CIs or demand new agreements that would protect academic freedoms:

> Confucius Institutes function as an arm of the Chinese state and are allowed to ignore academic freedom. Their academic activities are under the supervision of Hanban, a Chinese state agency which is chaired by a member of the Politburo and the vice-premier of the People's Republic of China. Most agreements establishing Confucius Institutes feature nondisclosure clauses and unacceptable concessions to the political aims and practices of the government of China. Specifically, North American universities permit Confucius Institutes to advance a state agenda in the recruitment and control of academic staff, in the choice of curriculum, and the restriction of debate.

That criticism has started to take root, and some institutions are beginning to banish these propaganda-filled centers. This won't make American universities completely free of Chinese influence and potential censorship, though. China has another method of holding sway over American universities, if it chooses to use it.

Infiltration by Tuition

More than 350,000 Chinese students were enrolled in US universities in 2017. That means that 32.5 percent of the total 1.08 million international college students in the United States were from China. Since annual tuition fees for state institutions average about $25,000 and fees for private colleges average about $35,000 (and counting), let's assume these Chinese students each pay $30,000. That's more than $10 billion being pumped into the US higher education system. Every year. And considering that that figure doesn't factor in room, board, travel, or entertainment, it's safe to say China's college students generate a $15–20 billion windfall ever year to schools and their communities.

China has a vested interest in sending its students here. For one thing, the United States is regarded as having the best higher education system in the world. For another, sending students here is part and parcel of China's goal to obtain technology. Chinese students are contacted by diplomats and business representatives and instructed to obtain useful technology. But suppose a school like New York University—the most popular higher education destination for Chinese students in the United States, with an estimated three thousand enrolled annually—hires leading dissidents and outspoken critics of Beijing to teach classes. What if China threatens to pull all funding for Chinese students at NYU who pay, say, $47,000 in tuition for the private university? That would be $141 million in vanished revenue (plus millions more for room and board). Given that, if China complains about dissident professors or curriculum that is critical of China's policies, do you think it will be heard? I've been told that this exact scenario has played out at multiple universities across the country.

The University of California at Berkeley has the second-largest population of students from China. A professor there told me he once spotted the Chinese consul general on campus and asked what he was doing there.

"Oh, nothing," came the reply.

The professor was curious. He followed the official, who then walked into a meeting of Chinese students. The professor watched as the visitor warned the students not to forget where they came from: "We are watching you, and you need to be good. You need to be faithful to China."

It might seem that welcoming Chinese students to the United States—and letting them experience a liberal culture where freedom of speech, religion, and politics is celebrated rather than persecuted—would be the first step toward creating opposition to the CCP at home. Obviously, warnings like this from political operatives are one reason why US universities are not churning out democracy-loving Chinese dissidents. In fact, Chinese students are advised not to fraternize extensively with American students and to maintain close contact with other Chinese foreign students. Given the Chinese government's thirst for monitoring individual behavior, there is little doubt that these students are asked to report on one another. So instead of enjoying freedom of assembly and freedom of speech—fundamental American rights—these students are haunted by the authoritarian rules of their homeland. With the advent of social credit scores—the newly implemented data collection system that monitors, punishes, and rewards citizen behavior—in China and the long reach of digital surveillance, it is quite possible that a Chinese student's liberal actions abroad could be used to penalize family members back home—or even result in having their funding cut.

The Chinese diaspora is another agent of influence for Beijing. An estimated forty-five million Chinese speakers are living outside China and Taiwan, with roots to the mainland, and the CCP continually appeals to this population in all manner of ways. To the Chinese government, this is an informal but potent network, one that appeals to family, ancestry, identity, and nationhood. These can be powerful manipulative tools. The CCP uses them to activate what they call "nontraditional collectors": foreign-born Chinese who can become diplomatic or intelligence assets. They are often spurred into action—providing information, stealing secrets, attending rallies, writing letters—by the win-win logic of their CCP handlers. That logic is twofold—it's based on appeals to the pride and patriotism in the Chinese nation and the idea that collectors can help themselves—by being a patriot or, maybe, by accepting a payment—and help the "homeland."

When I was working as the Defense attaché in Beijing, I flew with members of the PLA to a conference in Miami. The next day, the entourage caught a flight to New York. The PLA members of the contingent were sitting at the front of the plane. I was seated in the back, surrounded by a number of Chinese-speaking Americans. My seatmates looked like they had been beaten up. They had bandages and visible scrapes and even black eyes. *"Fāshēngle shénme?"*—What happened? I asked.

They told me they were members of Falun Gong and had been protesting the PLA presence and President Xi—until they were attacked and beaten by a swarm of Chinese nationals.

This tactic is deployed every time a CCP figure appears in the United States and protestors loom. A call goes out for all Chinese nationals in the area to mass in a show of support. But the other motive is to suppress protests physically. The Chinese nationals basically swarm around a protester, creating a barrier shielding them from prying eyes, and then pummel them.

Once again, China denies freedom of speech. Right here. Right now.

CHAPTER EIGHT

STEALING INTELLECTUAL PROPERTY

CHINA IS UTTERLY FIXATED ON ACQUIRING SCIENtific knowledge. It is a national obsession and has been for decades. Technology acquisition was important to Mao, who had his military obtain whatever Soviet know-how it could. It was even more important to Deng, who began the practice of sending students to the West in droves to formalize academic knowledge transfer. Controlling technology is given enormous prominence in the Chinese colonels' *Unrestricted Warfare* playbook, where, entwined with finance, it is viewed as a primary driver of influencing operations. Under Xi, the focus on tech hit a new high in 2015 with a ten-year industrial plan called Made in China 2025. According to China's State Council press release, the plan looks beyond 2025, codifying a "strategy of transforming

China into a leading manufacturing power by the year 2049."

Why 2049? Because that is the People's Republic of China's hundred-year anniversary, and 2025 and 2049 are nice target dates. But China has already achieved a remarkable level of high-tech success. It is unquestionably the world's leading surveillance state, with an estimated one billion cameras installed to monitor citizen behavior and its leadership in facial-recognition AI. China has the world's fastest supercomputer, the most powerful hypersonic wind tunnel, and the first quantum-encryption satellite communication system.

China is already the world's leading manufacturer, surpassing the United States in 2010. This is a reality that makes the wording of the Made in China 2025 press release—and its focus on becoming "a leading manufacturing power" in thirty years' time—a bit strange and deceptive. The plan lists priorities—improving manufacturing innovation, integrating technology and industry, strengthening the industrial base, fostering Chinese brands, enforcing green manufacturing, promoting service-oriented manufacturing—that focus on research and design growth. And a second list of "key sectors" makes it abundantly clear this plan isn't about upgrading conditions on the factory floor. It is all about developing cutting-edge technological enhancement.

Here's the list:

1. New information technology
2. High-end numerically controlled machine tools and robots

3. Aerospace equipment
4. Ocean engineering equipment and high-end vessels
5. High-end rail transportation equipment
6. Energy-saving cars and new-energy cars
7. Electrical equipment
8. Farming machines
9. New materials, such as polymers
10. Bio-medicine and high-end medical equipment

Controlling the design and manufacturing of these sectors is a means to an end. It is the critical first step to subsuming and/or dominating companies across the globe. Once that is achieved—once China is the market leader in, for example, farm machines and medical equipment, and once it owns high-end shipping vessels and the ports to travel to—the economic levers of influence will enshrine its ability to ensure geopolitical control of vast swaths of the world.

This may sound "diabolical." It may seem like something straight out of a dystopian science fiction novel. It may even sound unbelievable, because, really, what kind of society could envision this kind of end-to-end power? But this is the plan.

To execute it, China has put technology transfer at the forefront of all its goals. So much so, it has now designated its entire population as spies. On June 28, 2017, the CCP passed a sweeping National Intelligence Law. It gives the government absurdly broad powers to monitor all people, as well as domestic and foreign companies and organizations, within China's borders. It also gives intelligence officers the right to designate businesses and individuals as spies. Here is the Spies "R" Us legal provision:

> Article 14: National intelligence work institutions, when carrying out intelligence work according to laws, may ask relevant institutions, organizations and citizens to provide necessary support, assistance and cooperation.

This is a very important development, and one that formalizes and provides legal cover for China's immoral, unethical, "whatever it takes" approach to obtaining technology. By establishing the "right" to "ask" its citizens to join in government-sanctioned "intelligence work," the CCP is sanctioning any and all citizens to acquire plans, data, intellectual property—anything, really—from anyone anywhere. And once again, China's newly installed social credit scores seem likely to come into play here, providing the CCP with another lever, if they need it, to incentivize citizens to comply with espionage requests or suffer the consequences. Imagine a Chinese employee of a foreign company in Beijing being asked to spy on his employers and being told their child will not be admitted to a certain school unless they swipe data. What's the harm? Its win-win.

Some intelligence work is relatively benign. The CIA has hundreds of analysts who have more in common with economics professors than with James Bond. These people track and study events, economies, political figures. But the CIA and its analysts are not, generally speaking, in the business of stealing corporate secrets about, say, Huawei and then handing them off to AT&T. With the CCP now essentially claiming the legal ability to, in effect, draft companies and workers to obtain technology, it isn't a complete stretch to say everyone can be regarded as a potential spy.

Ironically, on March 15, 2019, almost a year after the CCP reserved the right to make all citizens spies, Beijing began whistling a nicer tune. Evidently, the US-imposed tariffs, a long-overdue response to years of China's predatory behavior and one-sided co-opting of free trade, sparked a shift. Premier Li Keqiang, the second most powerful member of the CCP, announced a law to protect foreign companies. He said the law—which was not released to the public—banned forced technology transfer and illegal government "interference" in foreign business practices.

In theory, the new law will impose criminal penalties for sharing sensitive foreign corporate information, which would be a deterrent against counterfeiting and IP theft. Li positioned the moves as part of China's finally opening up the economy and leveling the playing field.

"If opening-up measures are being spoken of, then of course they will be honored," he said.

All this should be taken with a Mount Everest–sized grain of salt. China has issued empty pledges to change before. And as one businessman in the US community told Reuters, "What prosecutor is going to bring a case against a Communist Party official?" The answer is, unless rule of law takes root in China, no prosecutor will. The only way a party member would be charged and convicted of IP theft or counterfeiting is if a prosecutor received marching orders from Xi, Li, or another top party official.

The legal realities in China actually undercut any possibility of real justice for foreign corporations. One US businessman who tried to engage in litigation in Beijing told me Chinese lawyers are required to take a loyalty oath to the CCP: "My lawyer's loyalty went to the party before it went to me—and I'm paying him!"

To show you how entrenched the CCP is in technology acquisition and how foreign companies are essentially powerless to protect their intellectual property, their assets, and their legal rights in China, here's a case study that reveals how the CCP can and will sanction the total annihilation of a foreign company. But it's also a case study in how to challenge them in their own unethical, immoral game.

The Tang Travesty

In 1995, Dallas-based venture capital entrepreneur Patrick Jenevein took his first trip to China. At the time, Jenevein was the CEO of the Nolan Group, which primarily founded several energy-related enterprises, including a natural gas processing company. That firm's expertise in maximizing natural gas output had caught the attention of the China

National Petroleum Corporation, and Jenevein was invited to visit Xinjiang Province, the energy-rich area in northwestern China.

In 1996, Jenevein established the Tang Energy Group and set to work in Xinjiang. Soon the company moved from natural gas processing into electricity generation, using natural gas as fuel, a shift based on Jenevein's own experience. "We made more money doing that in the United States than anything else," he recalls.

This change in focus led to a new relationship. Big gas-fired power plants use jet engines to generate electricity. As soon as Tang put a jet engine on the ground, it found itself working with China's biggest defense contractor, the Aviation Industry Corporation of China (AVIC), which was eager to learn from Tang's expertise. A corporate behemoth, with 500,000 employees and 140 subsidiary companies, AVIC began working with Tang on airfoils—rotor blades—for wind turbines. Tang and AVIC started a joint venture called HT Blade in 2001 to make propellers for turbines. "We grew that from nothing to become the second biggest blade maker in the world," says Jenevein.

HT Blade attracted the interest of Kleiner Perkins, a top Silicon Valley venture capital firm. The partners began discussions to take the company public in 2009 with a valuation of about $1.8 billion. Tang had a 25 percent stake, which meant it was looking at a $450 million IPO payday.

Meanwhile, Jenevein decided to start a company in the United States to sell wind blades to international turbine companies like GE, Nordex, and others. When AVIC asked to become part of the start-up, Jenevein turned it down: "We said, 'No, you can't. You're not used to the commercial process here. It's really quick, and a governmental process just can't keep up with that. The laws are very different here than what you're used to, and you can't take advantage of the investment tax credits. So we appreciate that you want to work together. We consider that a compliment, but no.'

"Then they said, 'We'll bring 600 million bucks.'

"And we said, 'Yes.'"

In 2009, with China's minister of Commerce, Chen Deming, looking on in Chicago, an AVIC offshoot signed the paperwork to provide Tang with an initial stake of $300 million for the new joint venture, Soaring Wind Energy.

But the deal—which would have used AVIC's funding to build wind farms across the United States and a turbine blade factory in Texas that was projected to employ as many as a thousand people—stalled. Jenevein attributes part of the inaction to a CCP power struggle between Xi Jinping and Bo Xilai, the former minister of Commerce who was eventually stripped of party membership after a slew of high-profile scandals. AVIC, of course, is a wholly owned government corporation, so the paralysis of party members waiting to see who would come out on top seems likely to have affected decision-making.

It seems possible, however, that AVIC was just stalling for time while hatching an alternative plan. And eventually, that is what happened. Instead of joining Tang's new enterprise, the aviation giant launched a subsidiary to compete with Tang's new division.

"Then they hired our general manager. They diverted our tax credit financing, and they stole projects," recounts Jenevein.

The attacks on Tang didn't end there. HT Blade, the joint venture between AVIC and Tang, became a target. The IPO plans came to a screeching halt, and the State-Owned Assets Supervision and Administration Commission of the State Council unilaterally distributed HT Blade's cash assets to Baoding Huiyang Propeller Factory, says Jenevein. It also designated other state-owned enterprises, Sinoma and Zhongfu, to take HT Blade's market share.

From Jenevein's perspective, the state-run businesses of China had fleeced him in multiple ways. Tang improved the nation's ability to process natural gas more efficiently, it developed gas-powered electricity generators, and it broke new ground in both the aviation and renewable energy markets by improving airfoils. AVIC and the government's Assets Supervision wing had effectively stolen the technology, the established manufacturing infrastructure, the marketing and sales teams, and the profits. Then they had come to America with plans to dominate the new market that Jenevein had targeted.

Summarizing the CCP-sanctioned actions toward Tang is challenging. At first, listening to Jenevein's story, I thought AVIC had essentially redefined the phrase "hostile takeover." Then I thought, no, that term doesn't do what happened justice. It was unprecedented. It was a brazen, wholesale industrial hijacking of two companies that were potentially worth billions.

It's one thing for China to do this to its own enterprises—after all, it's a totalitarian state, and the CCP ultimately owns everything: every tweet, every yuan, every factory, every business within its borders. But that it would do this to an international business and technology partner seems to defy logic. Why would any foreign company ever do business with China again? I asked Jenevein what he would say to any American firm considering working in China or entering into a joint venture agreement with a Chinese firm?

"Know what you must protect, and protect it zealously and from every angle available," he said. "Thoughtfully balance perceptions and realities of market opportunity with the longer-term potential threat that a joint venture partner may become a competitor—one whose government provides tools to 'rebalance' a JV agreement without your knowledge and protect it once discovered."

When I remarked that this arrangement seemed to present foreigners with a high degree of risk and zero guarantees of reward, he delivered a brief sermon.

"Risk equals 'uncertainty of outcome.' Potential gain or loss associated with a range of outcomes can absolutely justify risk," he said.

Ever the investor, he added, "Risk includes doing nothing." Then he refocused on China: "Risk emanates from CCP's core leadership more than from any other vector.

Political winds shift in China. Now we're facing some of the fiercest headwinds. We'll see tailwinds again."

Listening to Jenevein's carefully calibrated recounting of his ordeal, spun in a laconic Texan drawl, it is clear he is a man of superior analytical skills. As a member of the Council on Foreign Relations and a twenty-year veteran of China's business world, he can come off as a master of CCP tactics. Indeed, few have experienced the government-backed onslaught that Tang has endured. He began to work with lawyers to challenge AVIC's unilateral theft. Finally, in 2014, Tang fired a retaliatory shot, initiating dispute resolution against AVIC with an arbitration panel. He expected a battle, and that is just what he got.

A year later, however, the panel handed down an award of $70 million. Three years later, Tang won a confirmation of that award in US Federal District Court. AVIC has challenged that ruling, and the case is now being considered by the Fifth Circuit Court of Appeals. If the original ruling is upheld, it seems likely AVIC will petition the Supreme Court to hear the case.

Chinese Lawfare

Jenevein's legal journey has revealed the ways in which Chinese companies try to exploit US law. It is in fact a form of warfare—lawfare, which relies on the Foreign Sovereign Immunities Act, an army of lawyers, the crippling costs of litigation, and China's own murky labyrinth of ownership and bogus accounting practices to drive corporate subterfuge and to avoid prosecution.

Typically, the first thing Chinese companies do is try to deploy the Foreign Sovereign Immunities Act to protect themselves against American companies. Predictably, then, AVIC's lawyers claimed it was a state-owned enterprise and, as such, had immunity from prosecution in the United States.

Tang's lawyers expected this defense. They defused it by establishing that the case was rooted in a commercial contract and that the contract itself stated that it was a commercial agreement. Regardless of ownership, the crux of the case involves a judgment of commercial contract.

Jenevein, who is not a lawyer, says American companies doing business in China can help themselves by defining any business contract as a commercial agreement. Doing so up front will save time and money. But even without that language, establishing a case as a commercial contract dispute has proven an effective way to dismantle immunity claims. "You would go to the judge, jury, or panel and say, 'Look, here's the contract. It's completely commercial. Judge, arbitrator, you should find that this is indeed a commercial contract,'" explains Jenevein. "One great thing about US law is that, generally, the system tries to get to the right answer."

But another critical element to Chinese lawfare is to delay getting to that answer. Chinese companies are funded by the CCP. They have an entire treasury behind them. Every roadblock or speed bump—every petition, counterclaim, filing request—they can put in their opponent's way wears out the opponent's resources. And this is their primary strategy: make companies hemorrhage cash on court costs until they can no longer afford to do battle.

When Jenevein and Tang were awarded $70 million, AVIC lawyers filed two suits against him, one in Delaware and one in California. For $70 million. Each.

"They try to turn the victory on its head by additional litigation," says Jenevein.

Fortunately for him, the Tang case has attracted investors, who are backing him in return for a share of the court award. So Jenevein has been able to counter the infinite resources of his rivals.

Interestingly, there's something else that drives Chinese firms to engage in lawfare, and it has to do with party politics in Beijing, says Jenevein. But decoding the motivations and decisions made by the party elite is a bit like going down the rabbit hole in *Alice in Wonderland*.

"China or the Communist Party doesn't just make decisions based on capital," explains Jenevein. "They make specific decisions based on political outcomes. And so a political outcome is more important to them than a legal bill. They don't care how much money they spend, as long as they protect the political careers of those they want to protect or as long as they torpedo the political careers of those they want to take out."

Seen in this light, a court case isn't just a legal fight. It may also be an extension of political jockeying in Beijing, where party members may grab credit—or cast blame—depending on the outcome of the trial.

Meanwhile, back in the courtroom, Jenevein scored another critical strategic win. "We pierced the corporate veil," he says, describing how his legal team was able "*to weaponize the legal alter ego theory*"—the idea that a corporation can be set up to provide a legal shield for a person or entity actually controlling the operation. The Tang legal team showed "how the subordinate unit that acted badly was related to the head unit of AVIC that had committed to us, and we took those two command changes all the way back to Beijing." Establishing that relationship disarmed AVIC's claim that it was not responsible for the actions that wounded Tang.

One legal skirmish Tang lost was in the area of evidence and discovery. Hamstrung by lack of access to the Chinese legal system and the inner workings and filings of AVIC (as well as Chinese lawyers who take loyalty pledges to the CCP), Tang wasn't able to specify the types of documentation it wanted AVIC to produce. Until China improves its transparency and corporate governance, this will be a hurdle for anyone suing Chinese firms. Still, Tang's case appears strong, having already won arbitration and in federal court.

"They're going to fight it all the way to the Supreme Court," Jenevein suspects. "And then, when they lose, it's going to be a devastating loss, because it's going to be the law of the land. But what does that devastating loss look like? We still cannot do anything to make them write a check. *No one will write a check, because it would ruin their political career.* So what we'll have to do, and we're doing already, is start to go after their assets."

Diversifying Technology Acquisition

So add bald-faced corporate hijacking and lawfare to the list of ways China steals technology and research. The other tried-and-true formulas include forcing tech transfer as the cost of doing business in China; via cyber penetration, as I've documented via corporate attacks; or by placing Chinese citizens within research universities, research labs, and corporations. But China has many other means of acquisition.

One official channel is the Thousand Talents program, which offers foreign experts under the age of sixty-five significant sums of money. "Foreign Experts shall enjoy the preferential policies of the Recruitment Program of Global Experts in terms of exit and entrance, residence, medical care, insurance, housing, tax, salary, etc.," says the program website, which specifies that experts must commit to working nine months of the year in China for three consecutive years. At that's not all: "A lump sum of 1 million RMB [renminbi] research subsidies shall be granted to each talent enrolled. A total amount of 3–5 million RMB research subsidies shall be granted, through employer, to those engaged in scientific research, particularly those in basic science research."

For experts in the West with expertise that China truly covets, money is really no object. One engineer who built jet engines for General Electric is a case in point. It is easier to go to the moon than it is to build an advanced supersonic jet engine. When this engineer decided to retire, a Chinese firm tied to AVIC offered him ten times his salary. He eventually turned them down, opting to work with the Air Force instead.

Sometimes China just goes directly to a technology company and initiates a contract deal. This is what happened when Chinese military equipment companies working with the PLA had problems getting its deadly intercontinental ballistic missiles, which carry nuclear warheads, to work. It approached Hughes Electronics Corporation, a division of General Motors, as well as Boeing Satellite Systems, and struck deals, which basically provided China with the intercontinental ballistic technology it needed to launch satellites and rockets—and *deploy weapons on American soil.*

You might think that no amount of profits, no boost to shareholder value, would justify such a project. But this, evidently, is what can happen when obsession with corporate profit and market share diminishes and even vanquishes common sense. Lured by bad actors and big-money contracts, companies break laws, become complicit. Our national security suffers.

Eventually, the US State Department cracked down on Hughes Electronics and Boeing, rocking them with 123 violations of export laws in connection with the Chinese data transfers. The companies were fined $32 million each. Hughes issued a statement of "regret for not having obtained licenses that should have been obtained."

CHAPTER NINE

WORLD DOMINATION VIA INFRASTRUCTURE

INFRASTRUCTURE IS THE UNDERLYING FOUNDATION that society needs to function. China uses infrastructure projects—building roads, railways, power stations, and telecom platforms—as unassuming, innocuous, but powerful weapons to gain influence over potential allies and rivals alike. "Infra-" means "below," and generally speaking, the foundations of our society are below the radar, largely taken for granted. The average person doesn't lie awake thinking about the security of our gas pipelines, the cost or importance of maintaining roads and sewage systems, or who controls shipping lanes or owns a distantly located port. But these systems are critical to our very survival. The wholesale breakdown or even partial collapse of any one of them would lead to catastrophic events almost immediately.

China has displayed laser-sharp focus on its domestic infrastructure, building massive, maximally efficient ports to ship its goods, and (as we shall soon see) mining the West's investment coffers to build multibillion-dollar ghost cities in a bid to spur potential growth. But infrastructure development is also one of the subversive centerpieces of CCP foreign policy. Building roads, railways, ports, power plants, and telecom systems for financially challenged foreign nations literally paves the way for China to influence and control not only the "beneficiaries" of this aid but the surrounding countries as well, since transportation is the key to controlling the flow of goods across borders.

Infrastructure warfare may be the most subtle and most corrosive of China's unrestricted aggressions. Though it is always packaged as generous "win-win" development deals, its ultimate goal is a bait-and-switch in which infrastructure is provided but full control of the platform is never fully given. It remains in the hands of Beijing.

Haunted by Ghost Cities

In 2017, one of America's leading logistics-solutions experts, John Moran, CEO of Pennsylvania-based Moran Logistics, went out to dinner in New York City with the head of a major European construction outfit, who was in town to check on his $400 million development project. At the dinner, they were joined by the managing director of real estate investment for one of the world's biggest banks.

Moran and the banker hit it off. They discovered they had lived near each other in the past and had a number of connections in common. Moran, impressed by his new acquaintance's youth and title, said, "I'd be really interested to know, given your position, what keeps you up at night?"

The banker didn't hesitate. "Well, it's only one word."

"What is it?"

"China."

"Why is that?"

"Our bank and every other major Western bank has put hundreds of billions of dollars into Chinese real estate, and we have no idea how we're going to get it back. I go to China for ten days out of every month, and every month when I come home, I'm sicker than I was the month before."

Moran has traveled extensively in China. His company is a leader in international logistics solutions and partners with multinational corporations. He considers himself fairly attuned to business and finance, but he admits that the rest of the conversation was a real eye-opener.

"The average American believes that the eighty billion dollar a month quantitative easing money went into the American economy," Moran says, referring to the financial crisis bailout that began in 2008. "It basically went into the Western banking system, which in turn loaned it out to Chinese banks. The vast majority of these funds, though, was loans to the Chinese private sector through the Chinese banking system, which enabled them to continue building massive amounts of real estate."

The CCP dream is to have a totally independent economy, similar to that of the United States during the 1950s, when the booming domestic economy was neither export nor import dependent, says Moran. China planned "to build their own completely insular economy, which was strictly able to stand on its own."

To do this, China began building entire cities. They have assembled one hundred and twenty in total, with most designed to hold between five to ten million people, according to Moran. "Imagine the scale of these cities being twice as large as Philadelphia and many larger than New York City. It's staggering." To help put this growth in perspective, it may be helpful to note that from 2012 to 2014, China produced and put in place more concrete than the United States did from 1900 to 2014. To do that, it raised cash on the international markets with Wall Street leading the charge, and construction went into overdrive. In 2018, Moran toured the country. What he saw left him in a state of shock: many of the billions of dollars the banker was worried about reclaiming loomed before his eyes in the form of uninhabited skyscrapers, apartment buildings, and manufacturing facilities.

"The amount of empty infrastructure is mind-boggling," he says. "You're driving along in the countryside and you look across a field and you see a skyline that's bigger than the city of Philadelphia—and it's nighttime and there's not a light on in the whole city. There's no one living there. You hear about these ghost cities. But then you see them in real life, you just can't imagine it."

Moran says some of the ghost cities he saw were still growing. Everywhere he looked, he'd see a crane in the sky, launching more buildings. "I asked my host, 'Why do they keep building? Where's the company that's going to go in that 120-story skyscraper?' And they wouldn't answer. They didn't want to talk about it."

Visiting Shenzhen's gigantic manufacturing hub, Moran was taken to a two-mile-wide man-made lake. The lake was lined by solid cut granite along the shoreline and featured granite bleachers that could seat tens of thousands of people. There was LED lighting, piped-in music, breathtaking landscaping, and a cushioned running track surrounding the lake. As Moran admired the development, and the 550 million square feet of class A office space enclosing the lake, he asked his host what he was looking at.

"This is our future technology area. Our Silicon Valley."

The place was 95 percent empty, but Moran left the tour with the impression that an entire city had been constructed to hone intellectual property—much of it, in his hosts' minds, to be inevitably stolen from the West. It would be a high-tech, digital equivalent to Chinese factories pumping out pirated goods.

Given that billions of Western dollars have been invested in constructing empty cities, what is the vision for filling them and turning a profit? If the buildings are empty, what is the point of continuing to erect more buildings, more roads, and more electric and plumbing systems to make them habitable?

Let's assume that investors in the West were told the apartments would sell for $100,000. That is a steep price tag in a country where the average annual income is estimated at $7,500. Combine that low buying power with the flood of millions of units—by some estimates, sixty-four million apartment units remain empty, along with billions of square feet of office and manufacturing space. On the open market the value of this real estate should, according to the rules of supply and demand, drop like a ton of bricks. (How overbuilt is Chinese construction? You could take every man, woman, and child living in the United States and move them into those sixty-four million open units and still have empty apartments to fill.) But since the government controls pricing, the prices remain unchanged. Moran believes that because the millions of apartments remain unsold, private sector developers will start to default on loans to the Chinese banks, which in turn will default to the Western banking system. In this scenario, the Western investors who have plowed cash into building these cities will end up taking a huge loss, perhaps losing as much as eighty cents on every dollar invested. They are the big losers.

Moran believes that this will be a heavy price to pay for Western institutional investors, such as pension funds, and that the Western banking system may be dealt a fatal blow. Meanwhile, the Chinese developers still have those sixty-four million empty apartments, which they now own, and are now written down to twenty percent of their original price. If the Chinese government allows private sector developers and Chinese banks to cut prices, millions of Chinese people will finally be able to afford the apartments and populate the ghost cities. The CCP will have provided millions of homes for its people at the expense of the West. And what do newly inhabited apartments need? Appliances: ovens, refrigerators, dishwashers, washing machines, dryers, lamps, tables, stereos, rugs, bookcases, TVs, computers, and on and on. And infrastructure: hospitals, schools, shopping centers, manufacturing, and office space will now be needed to support these new communities. So by creating housing infrastructure—funded completely by the West at a massive loss—the former ghost cities become, in Moran's words, "the catalyst to restart the Chinese industry and help them get closer to their goal of having that independent economy."

Out-of-the-Box Authoritarianism

At the National Security Council, I was invited to hear a presentation by a foreign aid expert with the consulting group McKinsey & Company, which boasts on its website that it helps organizations "create the change that matters."

I sat down and watched the consultant give a PowerPoint presentation about China and Africa with a cringeworthy title: "Dance of the Lions and Dragons." I had heard good things about McKinsey and its reputation for hiring the best and the brightest. So I gave the title a pass and hoped the talk would blow me away.

It did, but not in the way I had expected.

The consultant began with an overview that basically said, "No other country comes close to engaging African nations when it comes to trade, investment, infrastructure, and financing the way China does, and we think there's a great opportunity for the US to partner with Africa in the same way."

What followed was an examination of how China has become Africa's biggest economic partner. And what unfolded was what I would call a five-phase plan for transforming an underdeveloped country into an IT-based authoritarian state. To be clear, the McKinsey team thought they were highlighting market opportunities and "win-win" nation-building. But it was a case of not seeing the forest for the trees.

The first step in China's insidious method of seizing control of developing nations is to find a resource that is needed in China, like minerals or oil or agricultural products. So let's say the nation has minerals. China will begin negotiating with the government about building a mine. It strikes a deal.

Step two is building that mine and ensuring there is power and water in place so the mine can operate.

Step three involves getting the mined mineral to China. So now China offers infrastructure planning in the form of roads, railways, and shipping ports. And don't forget, you need power and telecommunications to ensure distribution runs smoothly. So China cuts deals to build those platforms, too. Now the skeletal pieces for an industrialized economy are in place.

Step four is where the presentation surprised me a bit. The consultant said China's biggest investment in Africa, at the time, was in manufacturing, not infrastructure. They're investing heavily in low-value-added manufacturing, basically shoes, textiles, and products that require a lot of labor. There is a lot of irony buried within this fact: China, the bastion of cheap labor, was now outsourcing and creating cheaper labor markets. Of course, nobody mentioned this disturbing implication.

Manufacturing growth leads to step five: urbanization. Chinese firms will build housing because factory workers have to live somewhere. All this leads, theoretically, to bustling economies, where workers can now afford things like cell phones. And governments can install surveillance cameras and other social monitoring technology.

At one point in the presentation, the consultant excitedly told the room about the $50 cell phones being sold to Africans. As I listened to him marvel at how telecom companies had even changed the software on the smartphone to take better selfies of people with dark complexions, I thought to myself, "Oh my God, they basically engineered this to deploy their IT-based authoritarianism."

And that is the long game: facial-recognition algorithms rely on data from the captured photo, so better selfies lead to better social monitoring. With all these elements in place and entrenched in a burgeoning new nation, China is now in a position to replicate the digital authoritarian controls it has honed at home. It can offer governments access to a full suite of technologies, including AI-powered surveillance cameras and social media monitoring systems for evidence of dissent. In a generation, China can build a fully formed, information/data-based economy and deliver the controls to the authoritarian leaders. Meanwhile, the CCP can install a feedback loop and ship all this data to China. This improves its ability to build more business and influence the population. As a model of antidemocratic social control, it is a terrifying strategy. As a model for nation-building, modernization, and economic exploitation, it is brilliant.

When the presentation was over, I asked, "Who did you interview?"

The consultant said they had talked with the business owners, who were all Chinese, and government leaders.

I said, "Did you interview any of the people?" I was thinking about laborers, political opposition leaders, teachers, members of the clergy.

And he said, "Well, every once in a while, I talked to a taxi driver."

In other words, all this research was conducted, apparently, to examine *business* engagement on China's terms. There was no concern for political or social issues like human rights, freedom of speech or religion, or democracy. There was no discussion of kickbacks to political leaders that might be enriching the few over the many. Or the impact on the environment. The team may have tried to study China's work in Africa, but it was clear they didn't understand a thing about China. The big story, the only thing that really mattered as far the McKinsey team was concerned, was that Chinese firms were projected to generate revenues of $440 billion in 2025 by expanding aggressively in both existing and new sectors. Again, it was all about dollars and nothing about sense.

It would almost be funny if it weren't so frustrating and scary. The best and the brightest had unwittingly created an eighty-four-page influencing playbook for how Beijing practices nation-building, to turn African countries into governments with Chinese totalitarian characteristics. A how-to primer for making money, consolidating power, and monitoring opposition. Ultimately, all these countries end up with is a win for authoritarian rulers and a win for China. Meanwhile, these rulers don't seem to realize that China is not just "sharing" technology; it is also embedding its ideology and its citizens within the nation *and* installing the levers—massive debt, potential blackmail, data surveillance—it will use to pressure the country to do its bidding in the future.

One Belt, One Road, One Empire

In 2013, President Xi announced the launch of two enormous, futuristic initiatives with names that conjured up images of China's former stature as a dominant global power. The projects were called the Silk Road Economic Belt and the 21st Century Maritime Silk Road. Their precise details were somewhat murky—how this multitrillion-dollar endeavor would be funded, who the charter members were. One thing, however, was very clear. The two names resurrected the term Silk Road for a reason: to project China's return to dominance. The old Silk Road was a network of trade routes that first surfaced around 100 BC, connecting the Han Dynasty to Central Asia, Europe, and Africa. Eventually, the cumbersome names of the two Silk Road projects were condensed into one. The plan was called One Belt, One Road for a while before becoming the Belt and Road Initiative (BRI).

What is the BRI? It depends on who you ask. In bold strokes, it began as a plan to link China to sixty-five countries in Central Asia, Africa, the Middle East, and parts of Europe by road, rail, and sea. The plan called for China to partner with these "emerging" nations to fund and build the infrastructure projects required to make this happen, which of course means building many of the same attendant systems—power, water, communications—that they facilitate in Africa. Read the State Council–authorized Action Plan from 2015, and Belt and Road comes across as a pure-hearted international project of brotherly love to aid developing countries and facilitate free trade. The joke, of course, is that China doesn't practice free trade. But the plan doesn't mention this fact. The statement suggests that the BRI will help change that reality:

> China will stay committed to the basic policy of opening-up, build a new pattern of all-around opening-up, and integrate itself deeper into the world economic system. The Initiative will enable China to further expand and deepen its opening-up, and to strengthen its mutually beneficial cooperation with countries in Asia, Europe and Africa and the rest of the world. China is committed to shouldering more responsibilities and obligations within its capabilities, and making greater contributions to the peace and development of mankind.

But talk to Nadège Rolland, who spent twenty years as a China strategy analyst for the French Ministry of Defense and is currently a senior fellow for political and security affairs at the National Bureau of Asian Research, and you will get a dramatically different perspective on the initiative.

"Belt and Road is an instrument of political warfare," said Rolland, author of the excellent *China's Eurasian Century? Political and Strategic Implications of the Belt and Road Initiative.* "It's a tool. There's an infrastructure-building component. But you need to differentiate between what the propaganda campaign tells you and what it is in reality. So the propaganda campaign presents Belt and Road as a great open, inclusive, win-win endeavor for world development, economic development, regional prosperity, and things like that. The reality is that it's very narrowly focused on China's own interests, and it's an instrument to serve the main objective, with China's unchallenged rise."

Initially, Xi's 2013 announcement did not send tremors of concern through the corridors of power in the West. But Rolland was intrigued. Fluent in Chinese, she pored over any documents she could get her hands on regarding the BRI and spent time conducting what she calls "the double translation"—that is, looking at what China is saying about the project publicly, what strategies those words are cloaking, and what it is actually doing. "It's not just knowing the words in a different language. It's also what they mean, exactly," she says.

Adding yet another layer to her studies is the West's response. "It's not that China hides much of what they want to do; it's that outside observers don't seem to want to hear what they have to say or want to take them seriously. This diminishes the reality of what's going on."

Some outsiders buy into the earnest message China projects. "The Belt and Road Initiative (BRI) is an ambitious effort to improve regional cooperation and connectivity on a trans-continental scale," reads the World Bank's summary of the project. To its credit, the bank's coverage notes that the BRI carries "risks ranging from fiscal sustainability to negative environmental and social implications." But that hasn't stopped it from committing about $80 billion for infrastructure development in Belt and Road countries.

This is all part of China's strategy. As it uses the West's

money to improve its own infrastructure, it wants to fund the BRI using multilateral institutions, such as the United Nations and the World Bank, to pony up the cash to fund its vision.

Rolland studies the language that China uses when discussing Belt and Road. Listening to her, it becomes clear that the narrative promoting the BRI is designed to reshape the global perspective about fundamental values that define nations and drive sovereignty. China, she says, is "really proposing a different view of what the world should look like and the way international relations are conducted."

That framework is rooted in a mashup of Marxist-Leninist and Chinese imperial history, says Rolland—concepts that value the power of the nation-state above all else. When it comes to shaping policy, everything must be processed through the filter of benefiting the nation and ensuring its dominance. Nothing is more important. Not the individuals who make up the state. Not human rights. Not God or religion. It is a form of nationalism in which party doctrine and party power are the only things that matter.

"It's something very different from what we are used to," says Rolland, noting that Western nations are, at least theoretically, egalitarian societies. "The world order they foresee for themselves is that they are on top of the pyramid," and the people and rival nations are subdued and pay respect.

"I read something recently that was very nicely put," Rolland says. "It was almost poetical. 'I think countries should be like sunflowers turning their head to the Sun.' That's how they see themselves—with China being the sun, obviously."

In sections of The State Council Action Plan from 2015, however, China is almost invisible. The document is packed with feel-good positivity that offers an almost utopian vision of the planet:

> Jointly building the Belt and Road is in the interests of the world community. Reflecting the common ideals and pursuit of human societies, it is a positive endeavor to seek new models of international cooperation and global governance, and will inject new positive energy into world peace and development.

One of the things that is so cynical about the document is the pumped-up use of the word "peace" when in fact the BRI is among the most subversive of acts of unrestricted warfare. Here's one last excerpt:

> The connectivity projects of the Initiative will help align and coordinate the development strategies of the countries along the Belt and Road, tap market potential in this region, promote investment and consumption, create demands and job opportunities, enhance people-to-people and cultural exchanges and mutual learning among the peoples of the relevant countries, and enable them to understand, trust and

> respect each other and live in harmony, peace and prosperity.

All this sounds great on the surface. Dig a little deeper, though, and other motives are revealed. China and its initial sixty-five other countries account collectively for more than 30 percent of global GDP, 62 percent of population, and 75 percent of known energy reserves, according to the World Bank. Those numbers are outdated, however, because the CCP keeps adding partners to its plan. And all those partners—with the exception of Greece and Italy, two of the West's more economically vulnerable nations—are far removed from the nations Beijing regards as its greatest competitors: the United States, Germany, England, France, India, South Korea, Australia, Canada.

"When you look at the map of Belt and Road countries," says Rolland, "it covers two-thirds of the world and focuses on emerging countries. The way China looks at it, this is the future, because this is where the population growth is going to be the highest and where there's a potential to create a growing middle class. So they're going to flood the market with Chinese products, but they are also going to have access to the data, and that's really key for the future of technology.

"So, you see, it's not that they're looking in the past, focusing on railways. They are clearly looking into the future. Everyone is stuck on China building infrastructure and transportation infrastructure. They don't see that there's an entire category that they don't look at: big data and technology. What I find very concerning is that the virtual side of Belt and Road is, to my mind, more important than the physical connections."

Data and technology provide the most chillingly efficient authoritarian weapons for controlling populations. Data can reveal what you're saying, reading, watching, buying. It can reveal where you are going, how long you stay there, and who you meet. Data can be used for business and marketing purposes. It can be used to shape your opinions. And that, as Rolland indicates, will allow China to flood markets with relevant products—and then influence you to buy them. But data won't just allow targeting and influencing. It will also allow silencing. Data analysis will help identify whomever the state defines as bad actors. And technology will help find them. This is the end game of Belt and Road; it's not just about the free movement of goods and raising the standard of living—although it is, in part, about that. But that's the bait. The insidious switch, however, is that along with those supposed improvements, the BRI is also about restricting the movement of ideas, constraining ideological freedom, and removing any opposition to the authority of the state.

Rolland says you can see China maneuvering to shift values and perspectives in the way its diplomats frame policy: "It's like *Invasion of the Body Snatchers*. They have substituted Belt and Road diplo-speak into United Nations documents. It's amazing how skillful they are. So now you have Belt and Road mentioned in UN resolutions, for Pete's sake. That's something that people don't realize: language matters. And if you succeed in adding CCP tropes into resolutions or into UN documents, it gives that high level of legitimacy, and then they can use it to push their own agenda further."

In recent years, China has added South America to its BRI wish list. China owns the Panama Canal, a critical pass point for global trade, and the ports at either end of the US-made Pacific-to-Atlantic shortcut.

Shipping and harbor construction are a focal point of Belt and Road for a number of reasons. China owns around seven thousand merchant ships; America has around three hundred. The centerpieces of the Chinese fleet are the highly efficient Super-Panamax ships. These are massive floating delivery systems for Chinese exports. And Chinese-made ports are constructed to allow them to dock and unload at speeds that would shock American longshoremen. Logistics and efficiency experts have calculated that by increasing the load and unloading efficiency for millions of tons of cargo, the ships were able to cut delivery times in half. That increase in productivity translates into an increase in tonnage and, with it, an increase in profitability. But these ports, as mentioned earlier, may one day serve another purpose: providing operational bases for China's navy.

On August 21, 2018, China signed an agreement with El Salvador establishing diplomatic relations. A statement signed by Chinese state councilor and foreign minister

Wang Yi and Salvadoran foreign minister Carlos Castaneda said El Salvador agreed to sever relations with Taiwan. Wang issued a statement saying El Salvador would be a partner in the Belt and Road Initiative. Other countries have signed similar memorandums of understanding, including Venezuela, Bolivia, and Ecuador.

Although the United States is obviously not part of Belt and Road, Chinese businesses have made ominous inroads to control and destroy American infrastructure.

Operating within our borders, Chinese manufacturers are trying to derail our diminished American rail manufacturers by flooding the market with an oversupply of cheap railcars. They have been disturbingly successful at this. China Railway Rolling Stock Corporation, a state-owned firm, has won contracts from transit agencies in Boston, Chicago, Philadelphia, and Los Angeles by sometimes bidding as much as 50 percent below its competitors. Providing these cars, which deploy digital technology, gives a Chinese government–owned company numerous entry points to access information about municipal security—and the ability to control the operation of a vital piece of infrastructure our citizens and cities depend on.

Some countries are reportedly pulling back from the Belt and Road Initiative. China's treatment of its Muslim Uighur population risks alienating many partner countries with large Muslim populations. Meanwhile, what happened to Sri Lanka and its Hambantota Port is an object lesson in what happens when you agree to an infrastructure deal with

China: you are mortgaging your nation's financial independence and, ultimately, your country's sovereignty.

Loosening the Belt and Road

If anything in this chapter bears repeating, it's this quote from Nadège Rolland: "Belt and Road is an instrument of political warfare."

This cannot be stressed enough. Belt and Road is the geopolitical equivalent of the popular Chinese game Go, in which a player strategically places stones on a board to surround the stones of his or her opponent. When a stone is surrounded, it is captured and removed from the board. The player with the most captured stones and larger encircled territory is the winner. China is trying to infiltrate two-thirds of the world, an achievement that would allow it, in a sense, to encircle its rivals or cut off those rivals' access to other parts of the world.

CHAPTER TEN

SINO SOLUTIONS: HOW TO COMBAT AND STOP CHINA'S STEALTH WAR

THE UNITED STATES IS NO STRANGER TO WAGING economic and financial warfare. We've done it before. The collapse of the Soviet Union and the Eastern Bloc was, in large part, due to a series of little-known but hugely important measures enacted by the National Security Council that were designed to crush the Russian economy and bring down Moscow's totalitarian government.

One of the men who orchestrated this plan was Roger Robinson, the same man who stopped China Communications Construction Corporation from spinning off an IPO in Hong Kong. Earlier in his career, however, Robinson was a vice president in the international department at Chase Manhattan Bank. He was responsible for the bank's Soviet Union, Eastern and Central Europe, and Yugoslavia division in the late seventies when he wrote attention-grabbing articles about the trans-Siberian oil pipeline. His alarming projections regarding the future completion of the pipeline caught the attention of William (Bill) Clark, Ronald Reagan's closest adviser, and Caspar Weinberger, Reagan's secretary of Defense.

Robinson predicted that when the pipeline became fully operational, it would provide 70 percent of Western Europe's energy needs. That would bolster the Soviet Union's depleted coffers—exhausted by a deadly war in Afghanistan and efforts to match the massive US military buildup and the West's onslaught of technological innovation. It would also simultaneously increase Western Europe's dependence on the Eastern Bloc. Robinson joined the NSC, where, with the support of Clark, Weinberger, and CIA Director William Casey, he hatched a multipronged offensive to not only stop the pipeline but erode the Soviet economy.

"There were only about twelve people in the United States who were aware of this economic and financial offensive," Robinson says. "It was based on not just killing the second strand of the Siberian gas pipeline, but delaying the first strand by about three years and then denying official and, eventually, private credit access to Moscow."

To do that, the CIA, with the help of French Intelligence, obtained the KGB's wish list for American technology. Among the most coveted items were control systems to automate and maintain the trans-Siberian pipeline. Another NSC member, Dr. Gus Weiss, suggested helping the Soviets get what they wanted and booby-trapping their purchases with Trojan horse malware—computer software that would function correctly at first but eventually unleash destructive code. And that is exactly what happened: the system imploded, resulting in "the most monumental non-nuclear explosion and fire ever seen from space," Thomas C. Reed, former secretary of the Air Force and an adviser to Reagan and Clark, wrote in his book *At the Abyss*, noting that US satellites had picked up the explosion.

Many other levers were pulled by the Reagan administration, notes Robinson: "There was also a secret agreement with the Saudis to pump two million barrels of oil and decontrol domestic prices at the wellhead to drop oil to $10 a barrel." Indeed, with oil prices plummeting from $37.42 a barrel in 1980 ($114, adjusted for inflation) to such bargain prices, a vital source of hard currency income dried up for the Soviets. Meanwhile, Robinson and the government actively opposed any plans to permit the Soviets from issuing sovereign bonds, further depriving our rivals of urgently needed cash.

"It was the unsung part of a multipronged strategy of President Reagan's that also incorporated the Strategic Defense Initiative, the forward deployment of cruise missiles, the war of ideas led by Jeane Kirkpatrick at the United Nations, and the massive defense buildup administered by Cap Weinberger. And of course we went after them in the third world, with Bill Casey delivering Stinger missiles to the mujahideen as well as mining harbors in Nicaragua."

Limited access to much-needed foreign credit, an economy unable to compete in new technology, and the strategic erosion of the empire on so many fronts made it impossible for the Soviets to sustain their sovereignty. In 1991, the country defaulted on $96 billion in hard currency debt. Two days later, the Soviet Union collapsed.

Robinson believes that China is "a different kettle of fish" compared with the regime he helped bring down. But like other China cynics, he suspects that the world's second-largest economy is teetering on the brink of collapse. "China has immense vulnerabilities, namely this: it has a need to grow at an unrealistic rate while remaining a command authoritarian model economy that cannot start to withdraw the stimulus of new lending and publicly financed infrastructure projects and make-work projects. They can't get out of that vicious cycle, because to do so, although prudent, would have a devastating impact on the rate of growth."

Ultimately, China's shadow banking, market manipulation, and cash and credit manufacturing "cannot withstand the light of day," says Robinson. With nonperforming loans and debt structures now running at 300-plus percent of GDP, he says the numbers can't be sustained. "They're trying to pare it back, because they know they're facing a potential Armageddon, but they can't."

This is why Robinson predicts that accepted rules of the finance industry will defang the CCP: "Last time I checked, disclosure, transparency, risk management, good corporate governance, reliable statistics, share value, corporate reputation are all market terms, not national security terms, not sanctions terms. We're asking for the proper exercise of market principles." With this in mind, the United States must adopt strategies to impede China's campaign for global control. Our actions don't need to be as dramatic as the maneuvers that stopped the Soviet Union. They do, however, need to be focused, unrelenting, and immediate.

We need to ensure that fair trade is actually fair, and force China to comply with international trade laws.

We need to educate and incentivize Wall Street and captains of industry to stop promoting investment in China until it complies with trade requirements and accounting practices.

We need to invest in America—our infrastructure, our manufacturing, our R&D capabilities.

We need to ensure that 5G and all data in the United States is protected and secure.

We need to restructure, rethink, and reprioritize the US military to meet the challenges of warfare realities of the digital age.

In all these areas, our leaders need to do the one thing that others have failed to do over the past forty years: they need to take a stand.

A Line in the Sand

China attacks our economy every day in multiple ways. We have failed to draw a line in the sand. We need to support our businesses that are being attacked and having their intellectual property stolen through hacks. If a Chinese company is found to be using stolen IP, China must be penalized with tariffs, fines, and bans. If Chinese hackers are hammering at a government agency or a private company, we must be prepared to level sanctions that impact a comparable Chinese agency or business segment. If Twitter, which is banned in China, is besieged by Chinese influencers fomenting division, interfering with elections, and practicing psychological warfare, the Chinese version of Twitter, WeChat, should be prevented from operating in the United States. End of story.

Taking a stand requires a multipronged program that addresses the entire scope of the China threat. If there are no immediate reforms from China—and let's be honest, chances are slim to none that the CCP will willingly abandon unrestricted warfare and start playing by the rules—these policies must be put in place.

China uses financial incentives to create leverage. The West must do the same. Whereas China promises access to markets or offers of cash—the favorite tools of the CCP—the West must do the opposite in order to force China to stop its unrestricted war strategies. That means denying it access to capital and credit markets and sanctioning Chinese companies that do not comply with generally accepted accounting practices or that force technology transfer or are suspected of IP theft.

To do this, the rules of the free trade game must be

strengthened and the thirst for easy profits based on unsubstantiated and often fictitious valuations must be tempered. The mechanisms exist to severely deter investment in China. The SEC can and should use them.

Because every Chinese-owned company ultimately is controlled by the CCP, revenue generation and valuation of those companies is a fungible concept. Shadow banking is a given in China, where the CCP and its Bank of China can prop a company up or strip it blind. This reality makes balance sheets moot and accurate valuation extremely difficult. But it becomes impossible when you realize that China has barred the Public Company Accounting Oversight Board (PCAOB)—the gold standard of financial auditing—from inspecting the principal auditors' books of 224 Chinese companies listed on US exchanges. Those companies, according to *Compliance Week*, had a combined market capitalization of $1.8 trillion in 2018.

The heads of the Securities and Exchange Commission and the PCAOB started to take aim at this issue in late 2018; a joint statement warned that "if significant information barriers persist, remedial actions involving U.S.-listed companies may be necessary or appropriate."

The SEC lists three levels of assets when determining a company's valuation. Level one includes cash and cash equivalents from active markets. Level two consists of investments. Level three is for investment assets that are regarded as unobservable inputs—that is, investments that can't be reliably quantified because there is no reliable way to ascertain the value of privately held companies; companies that rely on shadow banking; certain mortgage-related assets; and complex derivatives. Because Chinese companies do not follow standard accounting practices, most should be considered level three assets. The Financial Accounting Standards Board (FASB) can institute this accounting policy change at the request of the Treasury Department.

If the SEC decides that the Chinese firms that don't comply with disclosure should be delisted—all $1.8 trillion worth of them—they will no longer have any significant valuation, per SEC rules.

Another possible move by the SEC would be to declare a company's nonconvertible cash holdings as level three assets. This would be a radical move. But it is certainly one to consider, to force China to stop rigging the system and cheating investors.

These SEC changes would likely result in huge losses for investors everywhere. Who knows how many millions GM has stuck in China from car sales there? Erasing those holdings would be a huge blow to the company's valuation. Yes, American companies and investors may be hurt in the crossfire. But ideally, the market for investing in China will cool and other markets will grow. With less access to investment dollars, China's economy will slow. Its ability to hit growth targets will falter. Its ability to fund international development projects will ebb. It will search for other income sources, and the United States must be prepared to apply pressure on other nations. Oil-rich Muslim nations—which should be furious over China's treatment of its Muslim Uighur population—must be encouraged to join the investment embargo and join the call for economic and social reform in China.

The China-boosting charlatans of Wall Street and the investors who listened to them will also be hurt. But that is the point: hedge fund cheerleaders and CCP enablers who have made hundreds of millions in trade fees need to wake up. Their actions have negative consequences for the future of our nation.

The portfolios of the fifty states' public pension systems are filled with stocks and bonds backing Chinese companies that should be flagged as bad actors—companies that build missiles or warships. These investments have national security implications, and investment managers need to start acting responsibly. This issue needs to become part of the national dialogue. Would American investors have invested in Germany during World War II? China's brutal human rights abuses—forced internment, denial of assembly, brainwashing—are eerily reminiscent of Nazi behavior. And with the use of relentless digital surveillance to persecute a population because of its faith, this oppressive governmental strategy actually deserves a new designation: post-Nazi.

These are tough options. But they are negotiating tools. Using them will force China to play by international rules. This strategy requires steadfast unity on a global level. It needs to be focused, targeted, and aligned with military precision, because, frankly, this is a war. Until these actions can be put in motion, hardball responses are vital. The three branches of federal government must use all their powers to protect our assets—technological, intellectual, monetary, and perhaps greatest of all, constitutional. It is a daunting prospect. But totalitarian China's cynical, antidemocratic, anti-individualist—*antihuman*—vision has left the free world with no choice.

Leveling the Playing Field

As we've seen, the CCP has no problem with Chinese manufacturers making counterfeit goods. And it has no problem shipping those goods into foreign markets. These bogus products generate income for China, put people to work in China, and, by undercutting pricing of the "real" product, wound the foreign-owned company that spent money developing the goods and bringing them to market.

Furthermore, China does not vet its shipments to the United States for pirated goods or goods made with unlicensed intellectual property—that is, patented processes or designs or software. The United States needs to stop waving these illegal products through its borders. We need to police our ports better, and we can pay for it by penalizing any bad actors we bust. For instance, if a ship from China is found to contain a single pirated item, the shipping company would be fined $1,000 for every container. Since the CCP owns these ships, some of which carry ten thousand containers, abetting piracy would quickly become expensive.

If that doesn't stop the overt smuggling of goods into the United States, then here's another idea: send the entire ship back to China. Yes, this would hurt the US companies awaiting deliveries. It might even create a shortage of certain goods. But it would hurt China more: companies would go unpaid, they'd miss delivery dates, penalties would be assessed, the shipping schedule would be thrown out of whack. The per-unit shipping cost of the goods—all absorbed by the shipping companies, presumably—would be enormous. It would be chaos and would impede the goal of Chinese shipping: to load and unload cargo at ports so efficiently, the delivery time of a shipment is cut in half.

Playing Hardball

On August 14, 2017, President Trump invoked the powers issued to him in section 301 of the Trade Act of 1974 and issued a memorandum asking the Office of the United States Trade Representative (USTR) to investigate claims that "China has implemented laws, policies, and practices and has taken actions related to intellectual property, innovation, and technology that may encourage or require the transfer of American technology and intellectual property to enterprises in China or that may otherwise negatively affect American economic interests."

Eight months later, the USTR delivered a scathing 182-page report establishing China's abusive policies toward US companies. Despite the formal legalese and business jargon, it is a fascinating document that confirms many of the points documented in this book. Here are just three highlights taken from the report's first section that expose the fully orchestrated campaign to force US businesses to turn over corporate assets in exchange for doing business in China:

- "Prior to 2001, China often explicitly mandated technology transfer . . . as a *quid pro quo* for market access." When China joined the WTO in 2001, it committed to abandoning that policy. "Since then, according to numerous sources, China's technology transfer policies and practices have become more implicit, often carried out through oral instructions and 'behind closed doors.'"
- China's National Medium- and Long-Term Science and Technology Development Plan (2006–2020) admitted the country's "relatively weak indigenous innovation capacity," its "weak core competitiveness of enterprises," and the fact that the country's high-technology industries "lag" those of more developed nations. To change this reality, the plan called for "enhancing the absorption, digestion, and re-innovation of introduced technology." As the report notes, the plan takes pains to spell out "the concept of introducing, digesting, absorbing, and re-innovating foreign intellectual property and technology (IDAR). The IDAR approach involves four steps, each of which hinges on close collaboration between the

Chinese government and Chinese industry to take full advantage of foreign technologies."

- From 2011 to 2016, on at least ten occasions, including four meetings tied to President Xi, China government officials publicly pledged to ease technology-transfer demands on American companies seeking to do business in China, and to ensure that all transfers were purely business decisions, free from government interference. There is no evidence that any actions were ever taken. In other words, all these policy promises were lies. It is worth noting that any demands for technology transfer in exchange for entry to the Chinese market are in violation of the WTO agreement.

The USTR report contains five more sections. These detail the following:

- The Chinese government's use of foreign-ownership restrictions to require or pressure the transfer of technology from US companies to Chinese entities
- How US companies are forced to "license technologies to Chinese firms on non-market-based terms that favor Chinese recipients"
- How the Chinese government directs "the systematic investment in, and acquisition of, US companies and assets by Chinese entities, to obtain cutting-edge technologies and intellectual property and generate large-scale techno-

logy transfer in industries deemed important by state industrial plans"

- How the Chinese government has conducted or supported cyber intrusions into US commercial networks to gain "unauthorized access to a wide range of confidential business information, including trade secrets, technical data, negotiating positions, and sensitive and proprietary internal communications"
- And the Chinese government's sundry other methods of acquiring foreign technologies, from hiring talent to enacting measures purportedly related to national security or cybersecurity in concert with inadequate intellectual property protection.

As this book was going to press, in June 2019, President Trump, frustrated by China's endless stalling tactics, announced trade tariffs on China. Predictably, monetary experts launched various predictions about the impact on both nations' economies. But from one perspective, it really doesn't matter. Launching tariffs marked an enormous shift in US policy toward China. For the first time in decades, a US leader told China that the unfair trade practices initiated by their totalitarian state were unacceptable. It was more, finally, than a warning shot. It was a sea change in policy. Of course, there had been a warning sign.

On Saturday, December 2, 2018, President Trump and President Xi dined together in Buenos Aires and agreed to a temporary, ninety-day trade truce during what Trump later described, via tweet, as "our long and hopefully historic meeting."

That same night, seven thousand miles away in Vancouver, Canada, an unexpected but arguably far more historic meeting was taking place between agents from the Canadian Justice Department and the chief financial officer and vice chairman of the Chinese telecom Huawei, Meng Wanzhou.

The agents placed Meng under arrest and announced plans to extradite her to New York, where she was to face charges for Huawei's alleged violations of economic sanctions against Iran.

On the surface, the arrest was a result of US Justice Department charges that Huawei had violated export laws by deploying technology licensed from the United States for use in Iran. But going after Meng, the daughter of Huawei founder and PLA military technologist Ren Zhengfei, was a dramatic move—another potential game changer. For the first time in decades, the US government took meaningful legal action against a company that is a bad actor. And not just any company. Huawei is the largest manufacturer of telecommunications equipment in the world and the second-largest manufacturer of cell phones.

It is also hell-bent on becoming the global leader in 5G networking, reportedly pouring as much as $20 billion into research and design for the next-generation platform. Seen in that light, the arrest of CFO Meng can be interpreted as something of a warning shot, a follow-up to the USTR report and a symbolic line in the sand.

Many intelligence and foreign policy experts view Chinese telecom and smartphone companies—Huawei, ZTE, Xiaomi, Vivo, Oppo, Lenovo, among others—as potential data-vacuuming tools for the CCP. Concerns that Huawei components contain "backdoor" programs to relay information to China have resulted in bans and stalled projects with numerous nations. Australia and New Zealand recently banned Huawei from working on networking platforms in those countries, and Poland recently arrested a salesman for the company, Wang Weijing, on espionage charges, which Huawei has predictably condemned. It has also denied any knowledge of its employee's activities or, for that matter, any wrongdoing on the part of Meng.

I have already discussed 5G issues extensively. But it's a drum that deserves repeated beating. When we discuss technology transfer—actually, when we discuss any data transfer—nothing poses a bigger threat to national security, to fair trade, to privacy and national sovereignty, than employing Chinese firms to run the system on which all digital information travels. It is, given China's stated goals and quest for technological superiority, the clearest and most present danger imaginable to democracy and a free world. And any country, any politician, any businessman, any investor, any citizen anywhere who can't imagine the repercussions of using CCP-backed telecom hasn't been paying attention. So putting Huawei and other Chinese technology firms on notice that the West will hold them accountable for transgressions and violations is a good first step.

The Trump administration also made a proactive move against piracy and unfair trade in 2018 that should leave A. J. Khubani, whose As Seen on TV business has lost countless sales to illegal knockoffs shipping from China, feeling better about his company's future. The Trump administration notified the US Postal Service of its intent to withdraw from the pact subsidizing shipping from China. That means American manufacturers can expect to see a reduction in pirated goods shipping via Amazon, eBay, and other open e-commerce platforms.

Stop Funding China's War Machine

In February 2018, the China Shipbuilding Industry Corporation (CSIC) listed a $1 billion bond on the Frankfurt Stock Exchange. According to financial investigators, the company arranged a convoluted paper trail for the deal, linking the bond to Postal Savings Bank of China stock and issuing it under a subsidiary of the China International Trust and Investment Corporation. Why mask the deal? Well, CSIC is building China's first nuclear-powered aircraft carrier—a state-of-the-art war machine—as well as nuclear submarines. The bond offering was, of course, available to US institutional investors—brokerage houses, hedge funds, pension fund administrators, anyone—and then made available on secondary markets. It isn't known who bought these bonds, but there is little doubt that some of the cash was American—and *it was funding the improvement of the Chinese armed forces.* Think about that. This goes back to the question posed a few pages earlier. Purchasing this bond, if you are an American, is the equivalent of buying German bonds during World War II.

This is a prime example of how CCP minions abuse Western financial systems and use Western dollars to strengthen the PLA defense systems. This, too, must stop. An interagency body should review Chinese and other foreign entities that come to raise money in the US capital markets. Companies and their subsidiaries would have to be vetted by intelligence, diplomatic, and military representatives. No doubt, the finance industry, fueled by trillions of dollars, would lobby hard against any investment restrictions. But if we are serious about making sure our capital markets are not used against us, we have no choice.

Similarly, cash from American retirement and pension funds has been used to stoke China's war machine for decades, as money managers use their members' nest eggs to invest in the China market. This means the funds of patriotic Americans, citizens with relatives in our armed forces, are being used to strengthen the enemies of our military.

Ideally, individuals who contribute to these pension plans should make their voices heard and lobby pension fund managers to divest in stocks that feed China's military. But it's a safe bet that most members of a pension plan aren't aware of the nuances of its portfolio. To build awareness and responsible investing, the government needs to create a campaign to inform our citizens of how US dollars are being used against our own interests. Lists of bad actor companies should be distributed to all financial institutions.

As far as stopping China from lording it over Taiwan, Vietnam, and Korea in the South China Sea, we now have a solution: asymmetrical warfare. That's militaryspeak for deploying unexpected tactics. With the termination of the nonproliferation treaty with Russia, we can build long-range and midrange ballistic missiles and deploy them with our allies. We can also deploy *mobile* missile units—the asymmetrical twist—which will prevent China from knowing where our missiles are. Together with an upgraded command and control system, we will go from an imbalance to deterrence. If China has no idea where these missiles are and they believe we have no compunction about using them—which is something we must convey—then we are in a position to prevent conflict.

The Nuclear Option

My biggest fear as we seek to balance our economic relationship is that the PLA is unrestricted. Therefore, we need the threat of nuclear bombs as deterrence. The assumption, of course, is that these arms will never be used. But invoking fear of the unthinkable—the madman or wild man theory of negotiation—often works. Look at North Korea: Kim Jung-un, a puppet leader completely controlled by China (if

China shut its borders with North Korea, there is little question the nation would descend into chaos and starvation), has two bargaining chips—a massive army that threatens South Korea and a nuclear bomb. His threats to use that bomb have sometimes spurred negotiations.

By the same token, President Trump's unpredictable nature may actually help in this regard. A president who puts all options on the table, as scary as that may be, is a good deterrent.

Promoting the General Welfare

China's strategy has worked so well for several decades because it reinforces a narrative that is pumped out by American business schools. Increasing shareholder value is the first commandment of building fiscal strength, period. This philosophy feeds into China's strategy because they use it to justify continued investment in their economy and in partnership with corporate America.

Since free trade leads to wealth and wealth leads to democracy, according to the misguided logic the CCP wants to promote, then tariffs must be bad. By allowing China into the WTO, the CCP was able to use reduced tariffs to garner American investment to grow its global empire. When tariffs were placed on China in 2018, that meant that lax regulation, poor environmental laws, and horrible employment conditions were not enough to encourage continued US investment. Unfortunately, when US investment goes to other countries, businesses often reward nations that emulate the CCP model by exploiting workers and polluting the environment.

This is how the CCP exports its model, by showing it works as a manipulative tool. Other nations copy it, and the free world continues to shrink. To stop the growth of totalitarianism, the tariffs on China and other nations that abuse international laws need to be made permanent. When that happens investment will flow back into the US. Already the US has some of the lowest energy costs, corporate tax rates, and regulation in the Organization for Economic Co-operation and Development. But corporations need stability, and they will not make investments in America and put Americans back to work unless they know they do not have a choice to go somewhere else where they can avoid following the rules for profit.

Until the tariffs are made permanent, countries like China will not start following the rules because they aren't penalized for doing so. Since corporate America only cares about maximizing shareholder value, they are going to argue against tariffs on nations that break the rules, because they need the higher margins that business in these sparsely regulated areas permits. This is how the unholy alliance between the CCP and corporate America was created and is perpetrated. It is also why American wages have been stagnant for decades and we have so many unemployed in the country.

Good Governance Starts at Home

Infiltration and influence are China's modi operandi. The CCP seeks to control outcomes by working within organizations and outside of them. It uses investment. It uses manpower. It is an insidious—and brilliant—setup that is designed to use economic power to achieve desired outcomes.

Because money talks, and because it is hard to prove that a business deal eight thousand miles away has affected a political decision in Washington, DC, policing Chinese influence is difficult. But there are a number of steps governments can take to limit the appearance of improper behavior.

Federal, state, and city government officials—and their families—should be subject to best practices. These would include making public disclosures about any ties to China or Chinese-owned companies. Ideally, politicians should be required to put their holdings in blind trusts while in public service. While this may be difficult and subject to criticism for being anticompetitive and restrictive, too bad. Nobody is forcing anyone to run for office or serve in the government. Members of the US military are held to higher ethical standards than our government officials. Adultery, for instance, is a criminal offense according to the Uniform Code of Military Justice. Given China's rampant influencing campaigns, US politicians and public servants need to be held to a higher standard for the nation's security.

To that point, congressmen should take a pledge to wait

five years after leaving office before becoming lobbyists. All too often, politicians run to K Street to cash in. They want to be influencers. They want to profit by shaping laws to benefit outside forces, including Chinese firms and the Chinese government. We need to be vigilant and reactive.

We also need to assure US businesses that government agencies will maintain their anonymity when they report a theft or attack—unless the attack jeopardizes consumer security from a data breach. These companies are being assaulted. Police protect the identities of assault victims, and our government needs to let businesses know that their identities will be protected if they report attacks.

A New Media Matrix

We need to develop Chinese-language media alternatives, both domestically and abroad, to combat the CCP's current worldwide monopoly on Chinese-language news and entertainment.

The goal of these alternatives should be to develop independent content that provides alternative viewpoints for the Chinese-speaking audience. Right now, China is piping an unopposed flow of anti-Western propaganda around the world. Opposition views, debate, free speech, discussion of democracy or religion—these things do not exist on government-monitored newspapers, websites, TV shows, or radio broadcasts.

The US government should promote and protect investments in Chinese-language media while shutting down all broadcasts of Chinese Communist Party TV and radio channels in the United States, as sanctions for China's flagrant violations of—pick one—international trade law, copyright protections, human rights, internet protocols, or standard accounting practices.

To keep incidents like the Voice of America scandal from silencing dissidents like Gong, the United States needs to relaunch the US Information Agency (USIA), a government agency created by President Eisenhower that is responsible for what is called public diplomacy. The VOA was part of USIA, but in 1999, the agency was shuttered and folded into the State Department, which practices private diplomacy. These two practices are polar opposites of the diplomacy game and should be kept separate. Right now, if China doesn't like what the VOA is doing, it can complain to the State Department and ask contacts there to use their influence over the VOA. Separating the two organizations would allow each to do what it does best.

The government should also close all Confucius Institutes and stop issuing visas to staff of these outposts of academic intimidation.

Immigration Alteration

The flood of bad actors from China is a systemic problem. Right now, immigration officers at the US embassy in

Beijing and our consulates in various Chinese cities have about thirty seconds to evaluate an applicant. This may sound ridiculous and implausible, like some sort of bad bureaucratic joke, but it is the truth. I witnessed the processing "process" as Defense attaché in the US embassy in Beijing. The immigration clerks face an impossible task. How can they interview prospective temporary residents and perform due diligence research to confirm visa applicants' identities in half a minute? They can't. The vast majority of applicants are simply handed ten-year visas.

China loves sending us their people. They see it as a win-win situation. It's another export for them of the one product of which they have a huge surplus: people. And many of them come to work for American companies, which not only pay salaries to these Chinese citizens but also provide them with access to American technology, American computer codes, American patents.

None of this is to suggest that every Chinese person who comes to America is spy on a CCP-sanctioned mission. It goes without saying that many are just hardworking people in search of a good job or a better life. And the issue here isn't some unbridled anti-Chinese form of xenophobia. It is, as I hope this book has made abundantly clear, that the CCP believes in and practices unrestricted warfare against the United States. We know the CCP sponsors corporate theft. We know it allows and promotes piracy. We know about its all-out drive to transfer technology from West to East. We know the PLA sponsors data raids. All these hostile acts were and are carried out by Chinese citizens. I am in no way suggesting we ban the Chinese from coming here or advocating a mass deportation of those who are here. But facts are facts. The State Department needs to devote time and energy to improving its vetting process. It needs to slow down and be thorough. Are visa applicants CCP members? Do they have CCP family members? Do they work in the telecom or technology sphere? Verifying the answers to these questions is essential if we are serious about protecting our country's resources.

One last ominous thought on this subject: by introducing social credit scores, China now has, theoretically and logically, another lever to influence and control the Chinese expatriate community in the United States. Chinese citizens could conceivably be pressured to forward corporate secrets, industrial designs, anything really, or risk having their score, or even the score of family members back home, lowered. Nine million people with low scores have been blocked from buying domestic airplane tickets and three million people have been barred from buying business-class tickets, according to *Business Insider*. Dog owners with low scores have reportedly had their dogs taken away. This is a powerful social control lever, and there is no reason to think the CCP won't use it to manipulate its citizens abroad.

Combat Global International Aid Loan-Sharking

While China amasses cash investments from the West, it is using that money to practice dollar diplomacy to influence the leaders of African, South American, Asian, and even European nations. The Hambantota Port in Sri Lanka is one of its most overt power plays. China-backed firms loaned money and services to construct the port and then, like predatory loan sharks, seized control of the entire operation for the next hundred years. But Sri Lanka is only one of dozens of developing nations that China is "helping" while clearly helping itself.

Rectifying this situation requires a number of responses, from diplomatic outreach to ensuring that US investments and nongovernmental organizations' loans to China are not diverted to pay for foreign aid projects. But our State Department and nongovernmental aid organizations also need to learn a lesson in nation-building. We need long-term engagement projects that improve society and develop alliances that strengthen local economies and increase democratic stability. Helping communities have potable water is great. But our aid should never end with one-off projects. China's model actually provides a good example of what US foreign aid and development should look like.

Congress funds water projects for different countries, but there is no overarching strategy for helping these countries develop and then connecting them to US markets by encouraging US entrepreneurs to build businesses. Unfortunately, US development projects frequently fail in this regard. Power Africa is a public-private partnership launched by USAID in 2013 that aims to light up Africa. It is a terrific idea that seeks to improve conditions in sub-Saharan Africa, where 70 percent of the population lives without easy access to electricity. The program has projects in more than two dozen countries, including Ethiopia, Ghana, Kenya, Nigeria, Senegal, and South Africa. But we need to be doing more than just building power stations and laying power lines. Chinese telecom companies have factories in Ethiopia. The Chinese built a rail line in Kenya and have reportedly been making inroads on constructing a new port for the East African nation.

We need to stop fighting and start building. We should take a page from the CCP's strategy and build up countries that can stand as arsenals for democracy in the region. It requires a concentrated focus on aligning democratic principles with free-market principles. Each step of the development process can help to reinforce transparency and openness. Meanwhile, if investment and growth opportunities surface during these aid projects, why shouldn't this activity actually benefit American entrepreneurs, since we are the ones paying? It makes no sense to enhance infrastructure and then abandon our work and let Chinese competitors reap the benefits. We need a strategy of building-not-breaking to generate profits for our development partners and our businesses that invest in them.

There are other economic strings that can be pulled to

help emerging nations and to shape hearts and minds to embrace democratic society. Former US ambassador to El Salvador Charles L. Glazer notes that in many South American countries, speaking English provides a significant lift in standard of living—and that just developing and promoting free online English lessons would be a major win. Meanwhile, when it comes to influencing operations, Glazer says that 20 percent of El Salvador's gross domestic product comes from remittances sent by Salvadoran immigrants in the United States. He believes that South and Central American immigrant communities in the States could help shape political realities back home.

Finally, the United States can and should reassert the Monroe Doctrine when it comes to China's activities in the Americas. For years, Chinese fishing vessels have violated international law by illegally trawling in our South American neighbors' waters. Some of these nations lack naval and coast guard defenses. By invoking the Monroe Doctrine—the nearly two-hundred-year-old policy asserting that the United States reserves the right to protect its interests in South America from foreign meddling—we can assure our South American allies that we will help patrol their waters and, if necessary, blow up boats engaged in illegal fishing. If this seems like a hard-line point, it is. China has demonstrated it has no intention of respecting international law or stopping its companies from overfishing—or stealing and counterfeiting—because it has not experienced any repercussions or penalties for the illegal behavior it supports.

A National Infrastructure Bank

When states and cities begin investing in infrastructure, they will choose projects and start accepting bids for these jobs. Until China opens up its economy, allows free trade, and stops breaking international trade law, no company with ownership ties to China should be awarded contracts here in the United States. It's that simple.

The idea that Chinese companies—all of which are essentially controlled by the CCP—should have access to the plans of our municipal transportation, water systems, or power grids is, to my mind, governmental malfeasance at best. But really, it borders on being traitorous. Awarding domestic work or handing plans to Chinese firms is an invitation to disaster. Ironically, the US government is urging other countries to be vigilant and cautious about working with telecom companies like Huawei. US corporations and local governments need to heed this advice, too.

While China has poured money and resources into its roads, cities, ports, airports, and industry, America's infrastructure has been crumbling. In 2013, the American Society of Civil Engineers (ASCE) gave America's infrastructure a grade of D+. Since then, very little has happened in terms of a national initiative to improve our roads, dams, drinking water, energy, and other vital systems. Not surprisingly, the ASCE handed out the same grade in 2017. America needs an estimated $5 trillion over the next ten years to rectify a multitude of issues. Despite the fact that infrastructural stability is essential to both our national economy and our national security, federal, state, and local governments cannot pay for it. Our once-robust national economy—which once provided a tax base to pay for investments in our communities—has been offshored, a victim of globalization. Our factories no longer hum with productivity. Our investment culture is focused on stocks and instant return on investment. Increasing "shareholder value" is somehow seen as more important than national security or our society's well-being. How, then, can we generate funds to make the improvements that are so greatly needed?

I have been working with members of the financial community on creating something called the Infrastructure Bank for America. Instead of leaning on our cash-strapped federal government for funding, we create an institution that acts as a low-cost lender and clearinghouse for infrastructure projects throughout the United States, both directly and through state and local governments.

Under proposed legislation in Congress (The Infrastructure Bank for America Act H. R. 3977), the board of governors of the Federal Reserve System would have oversight and supervisory authority over the bank. Here are the nuts and bolts of the bill:

> The bank shall provide: (1) direct loans and loan guarantees to private entities for the construction or maintenance of revenue-producing infrastructure projects,

> and (2) indirect loans and loan guarantees to state and local governments and state infrastructure banks for the construction or maintenance of infrastructure projects. At least 7% of the dollar amount of the loans and loan guarantees shall be for infrastructure projects in rural areas.

The bank itself will be funded by domestic and foreign sources, as well as private and government funds. One idea is to offer a tax holiday for repatriated foreign earnings used to back bank bonds and offer tax credits for initial equity investors in the Infrastructure Bank.

This is a private endeavor to solve a national problem. We need more of them to address the issue of finding the cash to fix our society. Infrastructure investment will pay enormous dividends for the United States: the projects will boost employment, increase national productivity, and improve the national tax base, as more workers earning more money means increased revenues at the state and federal levels.

There is a historical precedent for a national infrastructure bank. In 1934, New Deal legislators passed the National Housing Act. It had two goals: stop the run of housing foreclosures by providing access to cash, and spur home ownership and construction growth by essentially creating a federal bank to issue low-cost home mortgages, in the form of the Federal Home Loan Bank (FHLBank) System. America's housing stock went on a run that has never been duplicated. The act established construction standards and provided money to ensure that those standards were met. The result was the creation of the best housing stock in the world.

We need something similar. FHLBanks are private, with private funding and management. They are not subject to political influence and ensure a steady flow of funds into the housing industry. While one of the operating goals of the Infrastructure Bank for America is to offer low-interest loans for public and private development, I believe that money managers and corporations will see this as a steady opportunity—and a necessity—to invest in our nation's stability, standard of living, and security. Those returns alone speak for themselves.

READING THIS CHAPTER, it may seem, at first blush, that confronting the Chinese Communist Party's unrestricted war is an enormous and enormously complicated task. In reality, however, there is nothing to stop us from implementing these protections except our own division, greed, and complacency. We need to counter that with urgency, patriotism, and concern for our collective welfare. Here, then, is a distilled list of key strategic steps to help ensure our future and our children's birthright of freedom:

1. Discourage or ban investments in IPOs and bonds of Chinese firms or their subsidiaries, especially companies that feed the CCP's unrestricted war.
2. Create the market conditions for companies like Samsung and Ericsson to locate secure manufacturing

facilities in the United States. This will help ensure that no back doors through which to steal or sabotage communications are inserted.

3. Incentivize American investment in infrastructure and manufacturing in the United States. This can be done in multiple ways: by establishing a national infrastructure bank, offering tax breaks, backing industrial and infrastructure bonds, and making tariffs for rule-breakers and unfar traders permanent.
4. Regulate 5G implementation to comply with strict national security standards. We need a secure information network capable of encrypting all communications.
5. Immediately fund a C4ISR network, the state-of-the-art command and control system, for the Pacific, to maintain national security. Then begin manufacture and deployment of a mobile missile system with our Asian allies.
6. Create a government agency specifically to inform the civilian population, the business community, and our allies about the threats China poses to our democracy and basic freedoms. This agency should launch a national campaign equating fiduciary and investment strategy with national security. Corporate board members, stockholders, pension fund managers, and investment houses need to understand China's massive economic influence operations and their own role as enablers of our enemy. We need a massive campaign to create awareness that investing in China—among the most repressive, closed societies on the planet—is investing in tyranny. In the

age of fake news, disinformation, and hacked transmissions, we need to institute a way to certify documents and reports as authentic. One way might be a form of "blockchain"—a peer-to-peer program in which any changes to a document or program are listed on the document itself.

7. Prevent Chinese influence by creating an intra-agency clearance agency that vets politicians, policy makers, government workers, and foreign investors for connections to the CCP and its many wings.
8. Redefine our relationship with developing nations around the globe for long-term, collaborative engagement to counter China's Belt and Road Initiative. We must also reassert ourselves with regard to multilateral finance agencies like the World Bank and the International Monetary Fund to prevent China from using these agencies as their own piggy bank.
9. Forge a new consensus with like-minded democracies on free trade, democratic principles, rule of law, human rights, and self-determination.
10. Reinvent our military. We are spending too much on bombs and bullets. Instead, we need to shift our military spending toward infrastructure, manufacturing, STEM, and research and design. We should focus on 5G, artificial intelligence, and quantum computing.
11. Bolster the status of US Cyber Command. It should become the sixth division of our armed forces, joining the Army, Air Force, Navy, Marines, and Coast Guard.

CHAPTER ELEVEN

BEATING CHINA AT ITS OWN GAME

AMERICA AND THE WORLD AT LARGE ARE AT AN INflection point. China's stealth war is now entering its third decade of active measures. Its goal of becoming the dominant global power by 2049, one hundred years after the CCP took power, is now within shouting distance and seems within its grasp. America and the new global economy have been complicit, often unwittingly, in aiding China's rise. The good news is that China's plans are no longer hiding in plain sight. It is now up to our government, our politicians, and our financial leaders to act in the interests of our nation and the principles that have defined American society.

There are four key concepts that America and the West must adopt to thwart the CCP's lethal threat to our open society. But before I share them, I want to revisit one of the most critical and defining moments in American history. It will, I hope, provide a framework for and telling perspective on the challenge ahead.

On January 6, 1941, President Franklin Delano Roosevelt gave his annual State of the Union address. It was not so much an update on the state of America as it was an update on the state of the world under assault by Hitler. By summarizing the threats, Roosevelt was clearly preparing our nation for war. Privately, Roosevelt had long regarded the United States' entry into World War II as inevitable. He had urged Congress to lift the arms sale embargo to England in 1939. Declaring that the nation must become "the great arsenal of democracy," he had urged American manufacturers to prepare for war. Now the president was taking his case to the nation, using the speech as a tool to confront dramatic truths about Hitler's war on "the democratic way of life . . . either by arms, or by secret spreading of poisonous propaganda by those who seek to destroy unity and promote discord in nations that are still at peace." It addressed the dangers of isolationism. It even wrapped urgency in humor: "As a nation, we may take pride in the fact that we are softhearted; but we cannot afford to be soft-headed."

The speech's defining moment came in its closing minutes. "In the future days, which we seek to make secure, we look forward to a world founded upon four essential human freedoms," Roosevelt intoned. Then he listed them:

Freedom of speech and expression
Freedom of every person to worship God in his own way
Freedom from want
Freedom from fear

After listing each inalienable liberty, he added the phrase "anywhere in the world" to underscore the idea that these weren't just American rights. They were human rights, and every person in every country should be entitled to them.

This declaration, breathtaking in its simplicity and its scope, is why Roosevelt's address is now generally known as the Four Freedoms Speech. It was prophetic on a number of fronts. Almost exactly eleven months to the day Roosevelt outlined his vision, the Japanese bombed Pearl Harbor on December 7, 1941, and America officially went to war, fighting against fascism and for the freedoms that have been at the heart of our society. When World War II ended, Roosevelt's four freedoms became the bedrock from which the Atlantic Charter and the United Nations Charter sprang.

Roosevelt believed in a coalition of nations working together to ensure these freedoms. His speech even dismissed the idea of America marching alone to single-handed victory: "In times like these, it is immature—and incidentally, untrue—for anybody to brag that an unprepared America, single-handed, and with one hand tied behind its back, can hold off the whole world." Instead, he called for an international system characterized by rule of law and governed by peaceful dialogue.

The United States still supports the principles embodied by the four freedoms. Two of them are embedded in our Constitution. The world, however, has fundamentally changed. In today's fully globalized reality, we are seeing the fragmentation and destruction of a codified, principled system. Anyone charting the flow of money and influence across the planet will find national governments intersecting and competing on the international stage with not only rival nations but multinational corporations, nongovernmental organizations, criminal enterprises, and terrorist groups—all working at the speed of light in a free-for-all battle for profits, power, and control.

No nation opposes the four freedoms with the vehemence of China, and no nation has fed so parasitically on the globalized system to increase its economic and military power while appearing to conform to the rules and norms it seeks to undermine.

Freedom from want—the ability to achieve economic stability—is the only thing the CCP offers its own people. And while that particular liberty is a vitally important tenet that many in the West need to remember, it should never be viewed as the only essential human right. Speech, ideas, religion, the press—these cherished fundamentals of liberty are considered the enemy of the Chinese Communist Party. They are even specified in party literature as a threat to the enduring power of the CCP.

And this brings us to the last of Roosevelt's critical liberties: freedom from fear. The CCP, despite adopting an always amicable, win-win external message to the world, governs not by rule of law but by fear. It seeks to control its citizens, literally outlawing ideas, behaviors, self-expression.

There is little doubt that the CCP is eager to export its totalitarian vision of what people can and cannot do. It monitors its own citizens' behavior—social media posts and likes, purchases, emails—through digital means. And it monitors social media around the world. It is clear—or it should be after everything documented in the preceding pages—that the CCP will mine personal data across the globe to further its ability to influence and control economic and political outcomes.

Given the Chinese global influencing campaign and an ideological mania that advocates cheating, stealing, bribing, and repression to acquire economic and military power, there is one section of Roosevelt's speech that truly bears repeating. He is talking, of course, of the threat posed by Nazi Germany:

> I find it unhappily necessary to report that the future and the safety of our country and of our democracy are overwhelmingly involved in events far beyond our borders.
>
> Armed defense of democratic existence is now being gallantly waged in four continents. If that defense fails, all the population and all the resources of Europe, Asia, Africa, and Australasia will be dominated by the conquerors. Let us remember that the total of

> those populations and their resources in those four continents greatly exceeds the sum total of the population and the resources of the whole of the Western Hemisphere—many times over.

The same dramatic conditions apply today. Except that if our defense against China fails, you can add North and South America to the list of continents that will be "dominated by the conquerors." This passage is equally relevant today, because China's repressive treatment of its citizens borders on what can only be called post-Nazism. Its banning of religion, its surveillance and incarceration of its Muslim Uighur and Tibetan Buddhist populations, its surveillance of its own citizens at home and abroad, its jailing of dissidents, its focus on the supreme power of the state—these are all updates on Hitler's vision to control the world. The only difference, really, is that instead of blitzkriegs, military power, and holocausts, China invades and conquers by subversive means, harnessing economic power, illegal technology transfer, cyber aggression, infrastructural control, political chicanery, and, yes, upgraded military deployments.

STOPPING CHINA'S UNRESTRICTED WAR will take single-minded focus across the United States, and with our allies across the globe—the future of freedom is at stake. But winning this war means fighting it from within our own borders.

I estimate that we have three years to act. If the United States fails to disentangle ourselves from China's complex web of influencing campaigns; if we fail to curb our investments or solve our infrastructure problems; if we don't protect our citizens by providing meaningful work, or ensure the security and privacy of data with the same zeal that China exhibits to acquire it; if we don't rewrite the Foreign Sovereign Immunities Act to ensure legal protections for corporations doing business in and with China; if Congress and the Supreme Court fail to revisit legislation preventing cash from pouring into political campaigns to taint and influence the electorate, we will fall prey to Chinese policy at home and abroad. And we will, ultimately, lose the four freedoms.

China's actions to date have been cloaked in a web of deceit—just think of the examples cited in these pages of a worker being fired for liking a tweet, a controversial US government–funded broadcast being silenced, a congressman posing for a photo opportunity to pump up China's image regarding Tibet. But these subversive, anti-American acts grow more visible each day as the CCP gains confidence. Eventually, our politicians will become warped by China's infiltrations and the dam will burst. Yes, our Constitution will provide some protections. But that assumes that the political process can become immune to China influencing. And as we've seen, China will do whatever it takes to ensure the outcomes it desires.

In many ways, some of our leaders are already compromised. As I write this, Joe Biden is running in the 2020 presidential race. Anything he might say about a firewall between him and his investor son when it comes to China should be regarded with a healthy dose of skepticism. I say that with the utmost respect for Biden. I don't believe he would knowingly sell out America. But I do believe he is mistaken, like so many others in Washington, when it comes to China's end game and how it seeks to ingrain itself in our economic culture to obtain technology and political power—otherwise he would have urged his son to walk away from heading a Bank of China–financed investment fund. And lest anyone think I'm just targeting a Democrat, I refer you to the opening chapter of this book that details Republican Senate leader Mitch McConnell and his wife, Elaine Chao, the current secretary of Transportation—their relations with China are even more entangled and suspect than Biden's. The president of the United States—whoever it may be—needs to understand that China is the friendliest enemy in the world. A country that will smile and come bearing gifts for you—and then rob you blind. That's what it did when Clinton and Gore, Bush and Cheney, and Obama and Biden were in office. We need leaders who understand the duplicity and the threats—and will act accordingly.

The 2020 presidential election looms as an opportunity to seize the balance of power. To reshape America and protect the West—indeed, the entire world—from a totalitarian future where the four freedoms will not even be allowed to be mentioned. This is actually a huge opportunity for

America, a chance to reset and redress the investor-class decisions to abandon manufacturing and, with it, so many of our cities. As a matter of policy, making China a national issue and taking the necessary steps to defend our innovation, ideas, information, and capital will fix a great deal of what has plagued the United States for the past forty years.

At root, we need an overarching strategy driven by four basic concepts:

1. **Lead with Principles**—Asserting the legitimacy of the four freedoms, the United States must enforce—unilaterally if necessary but multilaterally when able—the rules and norms of the international trade system by withholding access to our society and economy or directly punishing those who abuse it. We will reunite free-market principles and democratic norms.
2. **Strengthen America**—The national infrastructure must be rebuilt, military superiority reestablished, borders secured, and people cared for, all while regaining control of our fiscal future.
3. **Organize to Compete**—The twenty-first century requires a government fully enmeshed in the information and digital age. That government must support and protect our innovation at all costs. It must be capable of detecting digital theft, piracy, financial abuse, and valuation fraud. And it must work closely with the private sector to ensure the economic vitality and security of our industrial base.

4. **Rebuild the International Order**—The idea of principled order supported by the four freedoms is fundamentally sound. It is today's international order that is unequal to the task of maintenance. The tools developed using the free world's innovation, ideas, information, and capital must be devoted toward the shared monitoring and enforcement that can propel the new consensus to permanent peace.

Our government, our political parties, need to work together. This is a nonpartisan issue. It's not about which party is in control. In Roosevelt's speech, which I hope every single candidate everywhere studies, he lays out his plan for the nation, specifically decrying the politics of division by repeating the phrase "without regard to partisanship" three times. A China strategy needs to be adopted across the board—by the president, the Senate, the House, the Supreme Court, and the people of America.

By creating infrastructure, by earmarking money for R&D, by mandating that certain products vital to national security must be manufactured in the United States, the government will enable job creation and technological innovation. By balancing environmental requirements with common sense enforcement, we can address climate change concerns as well. These policy changes will result in national dividends. The return of domestic manufacturing means we will rejuvenate local economies. And instead of being exported to pay for labor costs, money spent on local workers' salaries will remain in the United States, and some of it will be taxable. And that is okay! It will be used to create more infrastructure and to rebuild our military.

It's easy to forget that fighting wars has costs. Roosevelt laid that reality on the line:

> I have called for personal sacrifice. I am assured of the willingness of almost all Americans to respond to that call.
>
> A part of the sacrifice means the payment of more money in taxes. In my budget message I shall recommend that a greater portion of this great defense program be paid for from taxation than we are paying today. No person should try, or be allowed, to get rich out of this program; and the principle of tax payments in accordance with ability to pay should be constantly before our eyes to guide our legislation.
>
> If the Congress maintains these principles, the voters, putting patriotism ahead of pocketbooks, will give you their applause.

So an aggressive China policy will require political, patriotic unity. It has to. But that is just the beginning. Combatting China's economic warfare will require business *unusual*—a radical change in how our society thinks about fiduciary responsibility. Regulators need to reorder the incentive system so Wall Street, corporate America, and institutional investors will change the current culture and mind-set that focuses on profits, growth, and stock valuation as the only measures of success. That isn't to say the rules and motives of trade must be radically altered. It's to say that providing capital to China is a fool's game and, until things change, not only wastes money but incentivizes our competitors, who seek to co-opt US market share and earnings. Billions and billions of investor dollars are tied up in China. I've already told you the story of the banker who lies awake at night wondering how we will get our money back. He is not alone. Corporations—huge multinational institutions—that have leapt headfirst into China are faced with the same problem. They don't discuss the fact that they can't actually move millions of dollars out of China because if they did, that would upset shareholders and result in lower—sometimes much lower—valuations. That kind of thing costs CEOs their jobs. It also will cost investors billions in losses. Seen in this light, it becomes clear that pouring money into the Ponzi scheme of China abdicates fiduciary responsibility. Profits that exist only in China and can't be converted into transferable currency are not, in any traditional sense, profits.

There are other reasons powerful companies need to take their operations out of China. By moving research, development, and manufacturing there, they cede control of their intellectual property, which, as the past thirty years have demonstrated, will be stolen or co-opted. This, in effect, devalues the company. China's nonexistent environmental standards and worker protections also diminish the value of a company; it risks becoming complicit in worker and environmental abuse. Furthermore, as the United States does a better job of exposing China's sinister goals, these companies run a financial risk. If redressing China becomes part of government policy, as it must, it seems likely there will be a movement to divest in companies doing business there.

As for Wall Street brokerages, which make commissions on every and any trade—they need to stop cheerleading for China. Of course, brokerages have a vested interest in cheerleading. Every transaction results in a trade commission, and so new markets, new listings, new bonds mean greater earnings. But every dollar sent to China further enables their ability to be bad actors and destabilize the West. I've said it twice, but it bears repeating: Would Wall Street have floated German bonds during World War II? Would institutional investors have bought them? Never in a million years. Wall Street needs to acknowledge that the United States is engaged in an economic war with China and that by promoting investment in Chinese companies, which are ultimately owned by the CCP, it is funding the enemy. This may be an uncomfortable fact, but it is a fact.

If Wall Street will not police itself, government regulation will have to ensure that our citizens are not being cheated by financial institutions engaging in unfree trade. The SEC, Department of Commerce, the FASB, the PCAOB, the Treasury, the State Department, and the FBI will have to monitor the markets, the bad actors, the cyberattacks, the property thefts, and the piracy. China has engaged in these activities for decades—restricting the flow of capital, participating in accounting and valuation abuses, stealing intellectual property—with impunity. America needs a national policy to stop what can only be called "bad business as usual."

Wall Street trading houses aren't the only institutions that need to change. Our government agencies—the US military, the State Department, the intelligence community—must also transform themselves. The rubber stamping of visas for Chinese citizens must be stopped. Ten-year visas must cease. These visitors should be encouraged to celebrate America's freedoms, but they should also be monitored. And while that sounds awful, this is not America being repressive; this is America being reactive to a nation that has stated that all its citizens may be called on to aid Chinese intelligence operations. When China changes—when it plays fair, when it stops its culture of unchecked theft, of unrestricted warfare, of bullying its own citizens—then we can discuss liberalizing our immigration programs for Chinese nationals.

Meanwhile, as Roosevelt said, we can't do this alone. If the United States restricts capital investments in China, but European banks open their coffers, China will have no need to reform. Ditto for the oil-rich nations of the Gulf. So America must engage its allies and multilateral institutions and educate them about China's unrestricted war. It must work with like-minded nations to show the World Trade Organization, the United Nations, the International Monetary

Fund, the World Bank, and other organizations the unassailable evidence of China's hostile and often criminal bad-faith actions. Too often China plays at seeming compliant. But this is an act that masks a determined and calculated violation of international principles. That act tears at the fabric of the modern, connected world. It doesn't just destabilize the United States. No free state should involuntarily cede the bounty of its open society's innovation, ideas, information, and capital to a repressive rival nation that rejects basic human rights and seeks to prevent free competition in its markets.

I AM A FATHER. Like every dad, I want to see my kids grow and prosper. But I am frightened by the future. I am a former Air Force officer who pledged to serve my nation in a nonpartisan fashion. I still operate that way. And I admit that for a long time I was part of the problem. Believing China to be at worst a benign partner, I also hoped to one day do business with Chinese companies. After my Air Force career, I wanted to move back to Shanghai and, like everyone else, get rich. I am thankful for second sight. I used to scoff, like many, at critiques of our society that lay the blame for its many problems at the feet of big business or our federal government.

I don't scoff anymore. America was blinded by profits. As noted earlier, power brokers in London and New York decided to use slave labor in China to sell cheap products to unemployed people. It's snowballed from there, and China capitalized on a world driven by profits, greed, and the mantra of increasing shareholder value.

There is plenty of blame to go around. But I'm more interested in solutions. And if this book sometimes dwells on politicians or companies that have dropped the ball or missed the boat when it comes to understanding China, it's probably because I'm trying to explain how we got here. Or because I am beyond frustrated.

Our founders aspired to forge a more perfect union, and they gave us a guide in the form of our Constitution, which has allowed us to evolve over two centuries toward that more perfect state. I remain moved by the vision of freedom that has inspired this country.

That vision is now imperiled.

When finding markets, generating shareholder value, and growing revenues on an endless stream of stock and bond transactions become more important than protecting our birthright of freedom and our national security, we have a very serious problem.

I pray that this book finds an audience of Americans—and citizens of other freedom-loving nations—who feel as I do about the Bill of Rights and Roosevelt's humanitarian four freedoms. That is why I wrote this book: as someone who loves the miracle that is the United States of America, a country that celebrates freedom not just on July Fourth but every day as we live as we want, think what we want, love who we want, say what we want, and pray to whoever we want.

We need to work harder, faster, and smarter than ever before to ensure that we remain the land of liberty. I believe we can. But only if our leaders adopt a strategy that is more aggressive than that of our rivals, and only if we as a nation are prepared to sacrifice short-term investment fund profits and access to cheap goods for a future that guarantees our freedoms.

To me, the choice is a no-brainer. Actually, it isn't even a choice. There is only one way forward until China stops its relentless aggression: we must stop China's power grab at all costs or prepare to live in a society where the government can arrest you for possessing the very book you hold in your hands, or any book—the Bible, the Koran, the Bhagavad Gita, *Fahrenheit 451*, or *Winnie-the-Pooh.* Why? Because they don't approve of the content.

Because the very freedom to think has been outlawed.

ACKNOWLEDGMENTS

I AM GRATEFUL TO STEPHANIE AND OUR FAMILY, whose love and support made this journey possible. Seth Kaufman's voice rings loud and true in the pages of this book—all literary praise goes to him. I also express my profound respect and gratitude to the hundreds of people who spoke to me about this challenge to our democracy. I hope I have faithfully conveyed your concerns, insights, and pain. Finally, I want to express my respect and continuing partnership with all those both in government and out, who fight daily for freedom and the preservation of our Republic. Now and always, I have your back.